2004 POETRY

# ONCE UPON A RHYME

IMAGINATION FOR
A NEW GENERATION

## South East London
Edited by Steve Twelvetree

## Young Writers

First published in Great Britain in 2004 by:
Young Writers
Remus House
Coltsfoot Drive
Peterborough
PE2 9JX
Telephone: 01733 890066
Website: www.youngwriters.co.uk

All Rights Reserved

© Copyright Contributors 2004

SB ISBN 1 84460 451 9

# Foreword

Young Writers was established in 1991 and has been passionately devoted to the promotion of reading and writing in children and young adults ever since. The quest continues today. Young Writers remains as committed to engendering the fostering of burgeoning poetic and literary talent as ever.

This year's Young Writers competition has proven as vibrant and dynamic as ever and we are delighted to present a showcase of the best poetry from across the UK. Each poem has been carefully selected from a wealth of *Once Upon A Rhyme* entries before ultimately being published in this, our twelfth primary school poetry series.

Once again, we have been supremely impressed by the overall high quality of the entries we have received. The imagination, energy and creativity which has gone into each young writer's entry made choosing the best poems a challenging and often difficult but ultimately hugely rewarding task - the general high standard of the work submitted amply vindicating this opportunity to bring their poetry to a larger appreciative audience.

We sincerely hope you are pleased with our final selection and that you will enjoy *Once Upon A Rhyme South East London* for many years to come.

# Contents

**Brooklands School**
| | |
|---|---|
| Amelia Birrell  (10) | 1 |
| Sophie O'Dowd  (11) | 1 |
| Yelliz Ibrahim  (10) | 2 |
| Sarah Ball  (11) | 2 |
| Angus Clark  (10) | 3 |
| Mary Woodall  (11) | 3 |
| Katie Sheppard  (10) | 4 |
| Joseph Hall  (10) | 4 |
| Eleanor Johnston  (10) | 5 |
| Joe Wilkins  (10) | 5 |
| Joseph Smith-Morgan  (11) | 6 |
| Claudia Davis  (11) | 6 |
| Jasmine Castell-Thomas  (10) | 7 |
| Tiffany Hepher  (11) | 7 |
| Matthew Ashtari  (11) | 8 |
| Elle Marshall  (10) | 8 |
| Stephen Ellington  (11) | 9 |
| Talia Devito  (11) | 9 |
| Josephine Thomson  (10) | 10 |
| Roderick Pearce  (10) | 10 |
| Ronnie Raper  (11) | 11 |
| Ben Hunt  (10) | 11 |
| Phoebe Demeger  (11) | 12 |
| Jack Humphrey  (10) | 13 |

**Comber Grove Primary School**
| | |
|---|---|
| Jordan Blake Hancox  (11) | 13 |
| Victoria Sylver  (11) | 14 |
| Georgia Reid-Hamilton  (11) | 15 |
| Tanya Villiers Read  (10) | 16 |
| Alexandria Felix  (11) | 17 |
| Reiss McKenzie  (11) | 18 |
| Cedric Nyankomango  (11) | 19 |
| Cameo Montague-Raveneau  (10) | 20 |
| Priya Johura  (10) | 21 |
| Adetunji Oduntan  (10) | 22 |
| Francesca Anderson  (11) | 23 |
| Phuong Diep  (10) | 24 |

| | |
|---|---|
| Felicia Johnston  (11) | 25 |
| Carice Welch  (10) | 26 |
| Yasmin Chentouf  (11) | 27 |
| Isabella Hernandez  (11) | 28 |
| Kai Man Lee  (10) | 29 |
| Majid Kudsi  (11) | 30 |
| George Wade  (11) | 31 |
| Samuel Fagboyegun  (11) | 32 |
| Treya Picking  (7) | 33 |
| Darnell Pluck  (7) | 34 |
| Amran Sowe  (7) | 35 |
| Molly Petter  (7) | 36 |
| Chanyl Welch  (7) | 36 |
| Emefa Ansah  (8) | 37 |
| Debbie Boyo  (7) | 38 |
| Harry Locke  (8) | 39 |
| Rebecca Pritchard  (7) | 40 |
| Kit Pearson  (7) | 41 |
| Liam Walter  (8) | 41 |
| Anwaar Ali  (7) | 42 |
| Lêvyne Haughton  (8) | 43 |
| Adam Bouhlouba  (8) | 44 |
| Amber Hawgood  (7) | 45 |
| Ishmael Atterh  (7) | 46 |
| Amber Maurice  (8) | 47 |
| Rachel Sanguinetti  (7) | 48 |
| Ammarah Hamilton  (8) | 49 |
| Omolade Agoro  (11) | 50 |
| Emeka Orazulume  (8) | 51 |
| Devante Rodney-Francis  (8) | 52 |

**Dulverton Primary School**

| | |
|---|---|
| Freddie Price  (9) | 52 |
| Oliver Denyer  (10) | 53 |
| Mollie Selfe  (9) | 53 |
| Thomas Duncumb  (9) | 54 |
| Michael Burton  (9) | 54 |
| Sam Briggs  (9) | 55 |
| Yeliz Mustafa  (10) | 55 |
| Bryony Bonner  (9) | 56 |
| Kira Thorne-Smith  (9) | 57 |

| | |
|---|---|
| Ellie Custy  (9) | 57 |
| Joseph Coughlin  (9) | 58 |
| Jack Ward  (10) | 58 |
| Charlotte Avis  (9) | 59 |
| Alise Cotton  (9) | 59 |
| Ellie Barnfield  (9) | 60 |
| James Roberts  (9) | 60 |
| Joanna Sheldon  (9) | 61 |
| Alex Wade  (10) | 61 |
| Graham Frith  (10) | 62 |
| James Thomas  (9) | 62 |
| Sarah Wood  (10) | 63 |
| Joe Squires  (9) | 63 |
| Georgina Oram  (10) | 64 |
| Sian Qureshi  (10) | 64 |
| Sophie Moulder  (10) | 65 |
| Harrison Dark  (9) | 65 |
| Rosie Gillham  (8) | 66 |
| Joe Brown  (10) | 66 |
| Eleanor Minney  (11) | 67 |
| Mark Blaylock  (10) | 67 |
| James Dix  (10) | 68 |
| Nicola Gallagher  (9) | 68 |
| Emily Bruce  (8) | 69 |
| Lucy Carroll  (10) | 69 |
| Joe Sullivan  (10) | 69 |
| Jake Gill  (11) | 70 |
| Daniel Jenkins  (10) | 70 |
| Laura Curwood  (11) | 71 |
| Oliver Potter  (10) | 71 |
| Edward Healy  (11) | 72 |

**Foxfield School**

| | |
|---|---|
| Sarah Banks  (10) | 72 |
| Tanyia Beg | 73 |
| Ayodeji Akintinmehin  (9) | 73 |
| Ankita Dilesh | 74 |
| Connor Whitworth  (9) | 74 |
| Ruksana Begum  (10) | 75 |
| Mohammad Mirza  (10) | 75 |
| Annabelle Vuong  (9) | 76 |

Kelsey Ashley  (10)     77

## Heavers Farm Primary School
Latisha Francis-Rose  (11)     77
Kieron Nurse  (10)     78
Holly Eastoe  (10)     78
Stevie-Jane Watson  (10)     79
Joanne Boyd  (10)     79
Johannah Fening  (10)     80
Samuel Derek Willis  (9)     80
Zoe Charlesworth  (11)     81
Stephanie Allen  (10)     81
Ebbony Samuda  (10)     82
Rebecca Allen & Georgina Thomas  (10)     82
Ricky Dunn  (10)     83
Jenny Matthews  (9)     83
Rebecca Allen  (11)     84
Jordan Williams  (10)     84
Rea Lilliard  (10)     85
Chrissie Kiby  (11)     85
Sophie Wyllie  (11)     86
Georgina Thomas  (10)     86
Reiss Goodridge     87
David Layne  (9)     87
Karis Weller  (11)     87
Myles Shaw  (10)     88

## Holbeach Primary School
Neruja Sakthikumaran  (7)     88
Hassan Aktunch  (8)     89
Marcus Angel  (7)     89
Karling Morriss  (7)     90
Alana Falconer-Lawson  (7)     90
Rachea Allen  (8)     91
Soner Mustafa     91
Jessie Palmer  (8)     92
Phernell Davis-Senior  (8)     92
Lewis Stewart  (11)     93
Kirsty Hopkins  (8)     93
Shannon Marshall  (7)     94
Nadine Thompson Best  (7)     94

| | |
|---|---|
| Stepha-Kay McCarthy (7) | 95 |
| Brandon Carby-Wilson (7) | 95 |
| Molly Wole-Ajibode | 96 |
| Daniel Jeremy (8) | 96 |
| Abirami Thangarajah (8) | 97 |
| Bilal Butt (9) | 97 |
| Mpumi Nxara (8) | 98 |
| Lauron Macauley (8) | 98 |
| Nikita Miller (9) | 99 |
| Abbey-Gay Brown | 99 |
| Salar Rezaian (9) | 100 |
| Hassan Butt (8) | 100 |
| Gabriella Bent (9) | 101 |
| Sophia Elliott (8) | 101 |
| Natalie Palmer (8) | 102 |
| Rhianna Minott | 102 |
| Taylor Johnson (7) | 103 |
| Katie Talbot (8) | 103 |
| Nelson Hylton (7) | 104 |
| Lee Cornford (8) | 104 |
| Sarah Adebayo (7) | 105 |
| Joshua Reid (8) | 105 |
| Duyen Tran (7) | 106 |
| Dana Baines (8) | 106 |
| Gio Paris (6) | 107 |
| Boriana Ivanova (8) | 107 |
| Ashley Salmon (10) | 108 |
| Jake Miller (6) | 108 |
| Sophie Merrill (7) | 109 |
| Laura Williams (10) | 109 |
| Krystal Bailey (7) | 110 |
| Kavina Narayah (7) | 110 |
| Reece-Danielle Abbott (7) | 111 |
| Jamie-Lee Ingram (7) | 111 |
| Cairo Duhaney-Burton (7) | 112 |
| Zhané McKenzie (6) | 112 |
| Naomi Howell (6) | 113 |
| Théo Merlin (6) | 113 |
| Sebastian Elliott (6) | 114 |
| Liam Moroney (9) | 114 |
| Eliz Hassan (9) | 115 |
| Jade Angela Kidd (8) | 115 |

| | |
|---|---|
| Lorella Couch  (10) | 116 |
| Ceylan Mustafa  (10) | 116 |
| Ashley Lewis  (8) | 117 |
| David Welch  (8) | 117 |
| Makeda Roberts  (8) | 118 |
| Vanessa Adetunji  (8) | 118 |
| Kaner Scott  (8) | 119 |
| Michael Crawley  (8) | 119 |
| Samantha Sharpe  (8) | 120 |
| Avision Ho  (9) | 120 |
| Weronica Basia Bozzao  (8) | 121 |
| Tchaan Wilson-Townsend  (9) | 121 |
| Jade Beason  (11) | 122 |
| Georgia Farley  (11) | 122 |
| Paisley Thomas  (11) | 123 |
| Theo Batchelor  (9) | 123 |
| Kaileigh Green  (10) | 124 |
| Rosie Mgbeike  (9) | 125 |
| Lithasa Puvanenthirarasa  (11) | 125 |
| Echo Carnell  (10) | 126 |
| Yashar Aktunch  (11) | 126 |
| Tobi Olusola  (10) | 127 |
| Ellie Veale  (11) | 127 |
| Hope Mgbeike  (11) | 128 |
| Kieran Daly  (11) | 129 |
| Joshua Andrews-Smith  (11) | 129 |
| Caitlin Campbell  (10) | 130 |
| Lewis Lang  (10) | 130 |
| Lakisha Henderson  (10) | 131 |
| Hareesh Balendra  (10) | 131 |
| Dean Ferraro  (11) | 132 |
| Seun Olatunde  (7) | 132 |
| Lauren Lazic-Duffy  (10) | 133 |
| Nicole Lawson  (10) | 133 |
| Anaïs Merlin  (10) | 134 |
| Gokan Emirali  (11) | 134 |
| Sharna McKenzie  (11) | 135 |
| Amaju Ayonronmi  (6) | 135 |
| Emma-Louise Bullions  (10) | 136 |
| Jamila Francis  (11) | 136 |
| Savannah Harrison  (6) | 137 |
| Chelsea Scott  (6) | 137 |

| | |
|---|---|
| Sasha Agyeman-Dwommah (8) | 138 |
| Jensen Brown (10) | 138 |
| Melissa Virassamy (10) | 139 |
| Wajid Hassan (11) | 139 |
| Kieran Lang (7) | 140 |
| Kyle Mekarssi (10) | 140 |
| Tyler Cox (8) | 141 |
| Raeon McKenzie-Abbott (7) | 141 |
| Ernest Adadevoh (8) | 142 |
| Mariam Gul (8) | 142 |
| Ebony Okuonghae (8) | 143 |
| Omer Bozdog (10) | 143 |
| Danielle Lall (8) | 144 |
| Adetunji Iwala (7) | 144 |
| Rodney Abbey (6) | 145 |
| Otaigbeme Aburime (7) | 145 |
| Sean Gould (11) | 146 |
| Nicole Sandford (10) | 146 |
| Jazmin Devine (10) | 147 |
| Tereece Sewell (11) | 147 |

**John Ruskin Primary School**
| | |
|---|---|
| Ehab Ahmed (10) | 148 |
| Maxine Agyemang (11) | 148 |
| Sophie Walker (11) | 149 |
| Loretta Otokiti (9) | 149 |
| Jack Lawrance (9) | 150 |
| Ruth Boyd (8) | 150 |
| Romoan Oriogun (9) | 151 |
| Yohannes Kleih (8) | 151 |
| Alex Julien (8) | 152 |
| Tasnema Raaman (8) | 152 |
| Yetunde Adeola (11) | 153 |
| Nkemjika Eka (8) | 153 |

**Lucas Vale Primary School**
| | |
|---|---|
| Year 4 | 154 |
| Steven Viteri (9) | 155 |
| Sanchez Williams (9) | 155 |
| Ennock Tiemene (8) | 156 |
| Isabel Rodriguez (9) | 157 |

Temitope Ogundipe (8) — 158
Songhay Francis (8) — 158

**Montbelle School**
Lucy Sneddon (10) — 159
Alexandra Miller (11) — 160
Amy Watson (10) — 161

**Oakfield Prep School**
Tijan N'jai Sealy (10) — 162
Taylor Johnstone (10) — 162
Georgina Stenhouse (10) — 163
Victoria Dwebeng (11) — 163
Jack Brook (7) — 164
Maria Pittas (8) — 164
Henry Jiao (8) — 165
Hannah Warren-Miell (8) — 165
Sahara Patel (9) — 166
Angus Simpson (8) — 166
Talia Yilmaz (9) — 167
Nathanial Campbell (9) — 168
Amira Hasan (10) — 168
Ruth Eliot (10) — 169
Doris Dow (9) — 169
Gabriel Agranoff (8) — 170
Victoria Ewen (9) — 170
Christina Dwebeng (9) — 171
Rhiana Brown (8) — 171
Peter Leigh (8) — 171
Koray Yilmaz (11) — 172
Simisola Odimayo (9) — 172
Rachel Williams (9) — 173
Annabel Norris (9) — 173
Nagawa Kabanda (9) — 174
Joshua Martin (8) — 174
Emma Janusz (8) — 174
Rachel Rawlinson (9) — 175
Drewe Williams (8) — 175
Hamish Cooper (10) — 176
Freya Cooper (8) — 176
Lauren Wilmott (10) — 177

| | |
|---|---:|
| Jade Hermann  (9) | 177 |
| Jamal Edwards  (9) | 177 |
| Zein Harb  (10) | 178 |
| Samuel Kong  (11) | 179 |
| Ayesha Ellis  (8) | 179 |
| Kiman Xavante Hammond Read  (11) | 180 |
| Tara Collier  (9) | 181 |
| Shanice Saunders  (9) | 181 |

**Perrymount Primary School**

| | |
|---|---:|
| Brooke Hall  (11) | 182 |
| Nikki Thompson  (10) | 182 |
| Necla Diker  (11) | 183 |
| Jordan Stephenson  (10) | 183 |
| Poppy Franklin  (10) | 184 |
| Joe Sutherland  (11) | 184 |
| Mergime Shala  (11) | 185 |
| Monique Francis  (10) | 186 |
| Fay Simpkiss  (11) | 187 |
| Max Gallant  (10) | 187 |
| Shaun Johnson  (11) | 188 |

**St Mary Magdalen's Catholic School**

| | |
|---|---:|
| Scott Kirby  (9) | 189 |
| Margaret Obolo  (9) | 189 |
| Abigael Olorode  (8) | 190 |
| Nakeitha Monguasa  (9) | 190 |
| Ashlé Suckoo  (9) | 191 |
| Laurinda De Sousa  (9) | 191 |
| Kate Lodge  (9) | 192 |
| Christopher Douglas  (9) | 192 |
| Andrea Grillo  (9) | 193 |
| Denzel Uba  (8) | 193 |
| Sharma Beaton  (8) | 194 |
| Joanna Hernandez  (9) | 194 |
| Chloe McGivan  (8) | 195 |
| Holly Mason  (10) | 195 |
| Sophie Runnicles  (8) | 196 |
| Jordan Lohan  (8) | 197 |
| Lauren Barnden  (9) | 197 |
| Aaron McDonald  (9) | 198 |

Hazel Nezianya  (9) — 198

## St Thomas More RC Primary School
James Naylor  (10) — 199
Daniel Hickey  (9) — 200
Oliver White  (10) — 201
Shona Healy  (10) — 202
Millie Comis  (9) — 202
Amy O'Connor  (10) — 203
Matias Grez  (11) — 203
Yasmin Borg Ryan  (11) — 204
Alex Ahern  (11) — 204
Danielle Gough  (10) — 205
William Purbrick  (10) — 205
Emily Merrell  (10) — 206
Percie Edgeler  (10) — 206
Isabella Fayers  (10) — 207
Catherine Diales  (11) — 207
Frances Fitzgerald  (10) — 208

## Sandhurst Junior School
Callee Hart  (9) — 208
Katie Weller  (9) — 209
Caitlin Lawford  (10) — 209
Mark Muzzlewhite  (10) — 210
Balwinder Nazran  (9) — 210
Shebah Mimano  (9) — 211
Nicole Hemmings  (9) — 211
Sean Thurkle  (9) — 212
Jiselle-Loren Campbell  (9) — 212
Tegan Scott-Dobbs  (9) — 212
Christine Lyston  (10) — 213
Felicia Ayeni  (9) — 213
Brian Corfield  (10) — 213
Josephine Bourne  (9) — 214
Jordan Sewell  (9) — 214
Alana Watson  (9) — 214
Alexander Whipham  (10) — 215
Atalia Johnson  (9) — 215
Giovanni Ogboru  (9) — 216
Shanequa Hutchinson  (9) — 216

| | |
|---|---|
| Lemar Whyte  (10) | 216 |
| Paul Mitchell  (9) | 217 |
| Kajol Nandhra  (9) | 217 |
| Martin Ereck  (9) | 218 |
| Zeynab Mohammed  (9) | 218 |
| Aliye Giritli  (10) | 219 |
| Romario Williams  (9) | 219 |
| Helen McGhie  (9) | 220 |
| Stephanie Quirk  (10) | 220 |
| Lucy Ives  (10) | 220 |
| Jade Johnson  (9) | 221 |
| Efa Gough  (9) | 221 |
| Zephaniah Steadman  (10) | 221 |

**Sherington Primary School**

| | |
|---|---|
| Ryan Thornburrow  (9) | 222 |
| Ozde Yarseven  (10) | 222 |
| Dean Terry  (9) | 223 |
| Gethin Edwards  (10) | 223 |

**The Pointer School**

| | |
|---|---|
| Jack Beer  (8) | 224 |
| Max Higgins  (10) | 224 |
| Petter Austad  (7) | 225 |
| Adam Grahame  (10) | 225 |
| Ella Sofi  (8) | 226 |
| Rachel Chung  (9) | 226 |
| Heleana Neil  (7) | 227 |
| Raphael Newland  (10) | 227 |
| Nic Higgins  (7) | 228 |
| Anand Kukadia  (11) | 228 |
| Lien Raets  (7) | 229 |
| Danielle McErlean  (10) | 229 |
| Banisha Patel  (9) | 230 |
| Dionyves Martin  (10) | 230 |
| Chloé Saleh  (11) | 231 |
| Richard Samuel  (11) | 231 |
| Alexander Saleh  (9) | 232 |
| Mikaela Bere  (9) | 233 |
| Peter Currie  (8) | 233 |
| Eva Conn  (9) | 234 |

| | |
|---|---|
| Gabriela Saffer-Ford  (8) | 235 |
| Matthew Dean  (10) | 235 |
| Paola Delivre  (8) | 236 |
| Huw Jones  (9) | 236 |
| Mandy Ma  (8) | 237 |

**Thorntree Primary School**

| | |
|---|---|
| Josiah Adojutelegan  (9) | 238 |
| Francesca Latamsing  (9) | 238 |
| Steven Walker  (8) | 239 |
| Louise Case  (8) | 239 |
| Ross-Anthony Monteiro  (9) | 240 |
| India Golding  (9) | 240 |
| China Norris  (9) | 241 |
| Hannah Newman  (9) | 241 |
| Ben Khoshnevisan  (8) | 242 |
| Melissa Laurence  (8) | 242 |
| Josie Rogers  (9) | 243 |
| Nicholas Bulgen  (8) | 243 |
| Lucy Fair  (8) | 244 |
| Holly Spencer  (9) | 244 |
| Trevor O'Connor  (9) | 245 |
| Temidayo Olateju  (9) | 245 |
| Damilola Nezianya | 246 |
| Ndidi Aliago  (10) | 247 |
| Elizabeth Hogg  (9) | 247 |
| Emily Grain  (9) | 248 |
| Jake Moore  (9) | 248 |
| Callum Grant  (10) | 249 |
| Georgia Fair  (10) | 249 |
| Vishal Koria  (9) | 250 |
| Jessica McHugh  (10) | 250 |
| Jane Adojutelegan  (11) | 251 |
| Joseph Massey  (11) | 251 |
| Hayley Carey  (10) | 252 |
| Oscar Farmer  (10) | 252 |
| Amy Bowden  (10) | 253 |
| Terri-Anne Morris  (10) | 253 |
| Yolanda Allen  (10) | 254 |
| Lee Burton  (10) | 254 |
| Sonia Ahmed  (10) | 255 |

| | |
|---|---|
| Joe Perry (11) | 255 |
| Tom Hopkins (11) | 256 |
| Joel Moore (11) | 256 |
| Simon Dodd Wild (11) | 257 |
| Jason Summerfield (11) | 258 |
| Ria Berry (10) | 259 |

# The Poems

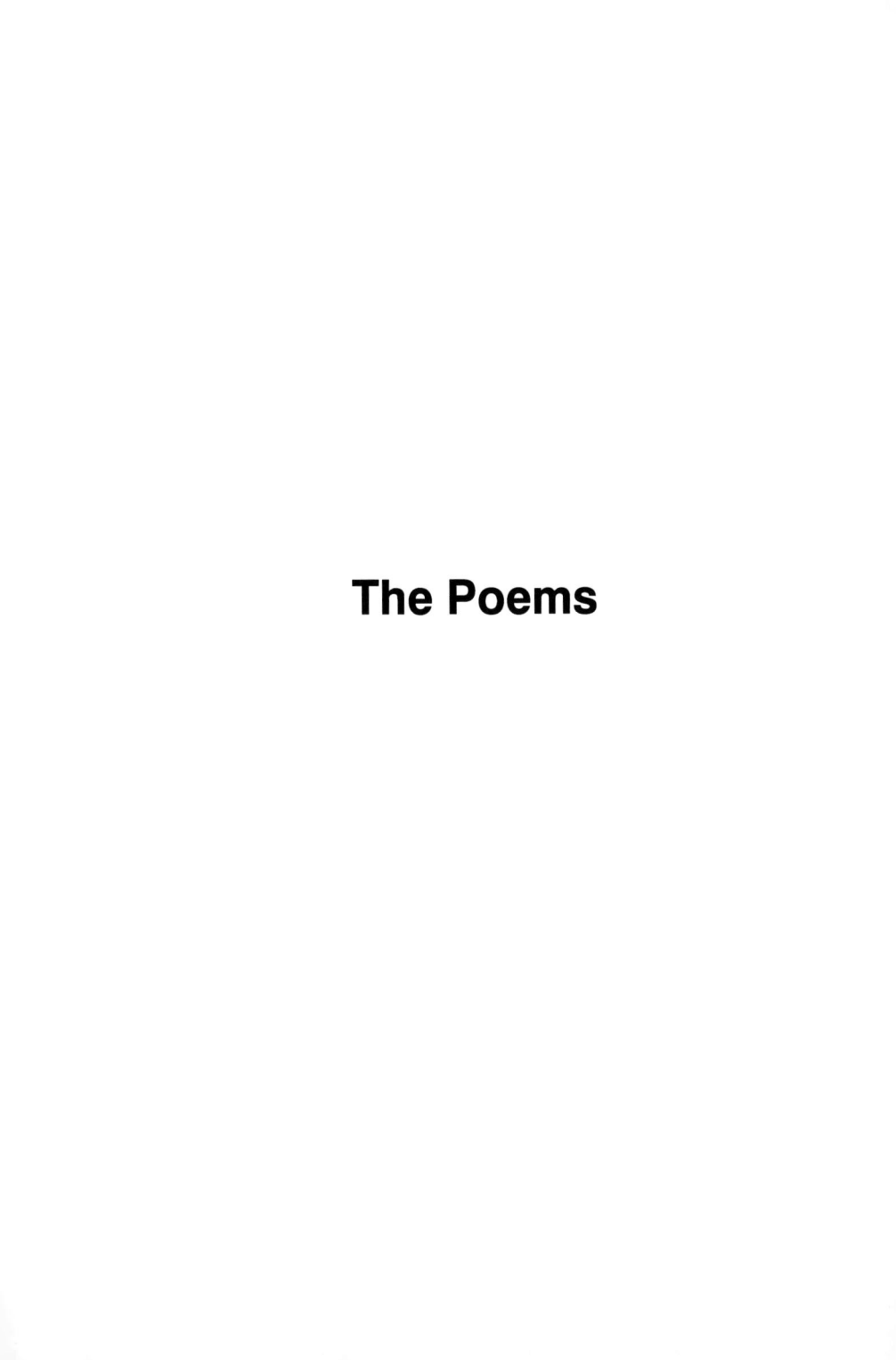

## Night

Night as black as black can be,
It comes, it comes so quickly.

But do you know how it comes?
For everywhere night is there,
There's a story to be told.

I bet you do not know how,
So I will tell you so.

One man will do a thing for us,
As they do every night,
As the sun goes down, something weird happens,
One man explodes and boom,
He dives in the sky.

He blows himself up but people don't know how,
With blue eyes and black hairs,
He creeps somewhere and bang - he's gone,
Just like that.

So that's what happens at night,
So take care, it might be you!

**Amelia Birrell (10)**
**Brooklands School**


## Waterfall

Off a river, faster, faster,
Bashing against the rocks faster,
Falling down a waterfall.

Standing at the top,
Looking down whoosh, whoosh, whirl, whirl,
Round and round it goes.

**Sophie O'Dowd (11)**
**Brooklands School**

## Suddenly It's Worse

Drip drip rain has come
Splash in the mucky puddles
Suddenly it's worse.

Watch out thunder's here
People rush to their houses
Suddenly it's worse.

Roads turn to rivers
Drains can't help 'cause they're blocked up
Suddenly it's worse.

Pavements cloaked with water
Water rising, rising now
Suddenly it's worse.

Raging angry sea
Debris floating all around
Suddenly, normal.

Dry roads are here now
No water cloaking over
Not a speck is wet.

**Yelliz Ibrahim (10)**
Brooklands School


## There Was A Young Lady From France

There was a young lady from France,
Who always was in a weird trance,
When disturbed shouted, 'Hey'
In the middle of May
And was never seen in a prance.

**Sarah Ball (11)**
Brooklands School

## Night

Night slips out through the door,
On to the open shore,
Where he covers the sea and sand,
With his ginormous hand.

Night ran onto the grass,
Where he wiped his dirty bus pass,
Where he yells for a ticket,
So he could see the cricket.

He makes not a fuss,
As he catches the night bus,
He travels the streets,
Each night he repeats.

His faces shines like the light,
Of the moon that is bright
His cloak sweeps around
As it covers the ground.

Night-time will end
As he reaches the bend
Around this finds
Light who he blinds.

**Angus Clark (10)**
Brooklands School

## Snow

Snow falls down on me,
So that I can't see a thing,
Like feathers in a breeze.

The breeze is like ice,
Throwing snow all around me,
It isn't very nice.

**Mary Woodall (11)**
Brooklands School

## Water Cycle

Five thin knives falling
Vertically through the harsh air
Splintered on the rocks.

Falls through to a stream,
Tumbles thrashing slightly
Finally calms down.

Hits the last curve,
Comes into the open air
Sea at last waves crash.

Throwing cold, wet foam
Swallowing small creatures down
Big waves like people.

Water becomes gas
Flies as high as winged creatures
Stops when it's compact.

Thin ones, thick white with
Blue, yellow, gold and cream splits
Comes a gust of rain.

**Katie Sheppard (10)**
**Brooklands School**


## Rice And Mice!

I once saw some curry and rice,
Which smelt so incredibly nice,
I sat down beside it,
I identified it,
As a bowl of curry and mice!

**Joseph Hall (10)**
**Brooklands School**

## Renga

Tumbling and gurgling,
Trickling and cascading,
Plunging into froth.

Winding forever,
Endlessly releasing life,
Rolling over banks.

Crystalline funnels,
Spraying out precious vapour,
Thaws of ice forming.

Winter is falling,
Glaciers take over lakes,
Icy air rises.

Icicles appear,
A fresh white blanket does land,
Snowflakes gently fall.

Snowdrops melt away
All life seems to reappear
Spring's open again.

**Eleanor Johnston (10)**
Brooklands School


## Winter Leaves Water

Ice begins to melt,
The streams begin to flow through,
The water warms up,
The fishes return,
The coral is full again,
Sharks eye the fishes,
The sharks will attack,
Smelling frantically for blood,
The fish are concerned.

**Joe Wilkins (10)**
Brooklands School

## Waterfall

Water gushing, splash,
Tumbling waves, rocky shores,
Splash on the surface.

Pebbles fly everywhere,
Falling from the shore,
Cutting like sharp blades.

As it falls from high,
Covering the ground beneath,
People stand and stare.

As the people watch,
They stare in great amazement,
They can't believe it.

**Joseph Smith-Morgan (11)**
**Brooklands School**


## Winter Falls

Rain falls from the clouds,
Blanketing the world around,
People stop and stare.

The rain makes puddles,
Frost beginning to appear,
The world gets a chill.

Sun begins to shine,
It melts the ice on puddles,
It evaporates.

I smile!

**Claudia Davis (11)**
**Brooklands School**

## White Water

Water, racing down,
Ice sparkling, galloping,
Watching water crash, splash it goes.

Clouds pull up,
The sea pushes out, splatter,
Pit, pat, a pear shape.

Bang, white hailstones,
Like tennis balls from the sky,
Harder and harder.

**Jasmine Castell-Thomas (10)**
Brooklands School

## Rain Cycle

Pitter-patter pit,
Little droplets coming down,
Droplets of water.

Puddles on the ground,
Ripples in the puddles,
I can see my face.

Water floating up,
Going up into the clouds,
To be rain once more.

**Tiffany Hepher (11)**
Brooklands School

## Night Poem

When it gets dark
It's in the park
What's it going to do
If it catches you?

It looks like a ghost,
Which people say most,
Its face is pale
And has a spiky tail.

When he makes everything dark,
He even does it in the park,
So what if you don't believe me,
I bet you tomorrow you won't see me.

I shall soon be dead,
Because night's in my head,
I'm warning you now
And don't say I'm a cow.

**Matthew Ashtari (11)**
**Brooklands School**


## There Was A Young Boy From Space

There was a young boy from space
Who bent down to tie his lace,
But then he found he was wearing a crown
Because he had won the Olympic race.

**Elle Marshall (10)**
**Brooklands School**

## My Renga

The stream is trickling
Downstream and tinkling as it
Turns thicker, faster.

The river gives birth,
White, foaming horses gallop
To the waterfall.

The roaring horses
Jumping from the jagged rocks
Now hit the bottom.

The winding river
Swirls through the river valley
Winding to the sea.

The white horses ride
Huge towering waves wash
Up and down, they crash.

**Stephen Ellington (11)**
**Brooklands School**


## The Space Dude

There was a creature from space,
Whose ears were too big for his face,
So he chopped off one
And put it in a bun
And never saw it encased.

**Talia Devito (11)**
**Brooklands School**

## Water Renga

Rising, rising up,
Joining together slowly,
Falling down again.

A slow, steady beat,
Falling, falling, never stops,
Breaking on the ground.

Deep two-faced mountains,
A stone hits, rippled they're gone,
Slowly gathering.

Raging, twisting, wet,
Twisting, turning, full of hate,
Clawing, craving, rage.

Falling softly and
Changing, changing hard and cold,
A puddle is left.

Cold against my face,
The Earth covered with silence,
A white, cold blanket.

**Josephine Thomson (10)**
Brooklands School


## Night

As night glides out
The lights go out.

He runs to a tree and looks at its leaves,
He tosses some dust and its light goes out.

With a pop and a bang,
Two more go out, then it glides away
From the two massive trees.

**Roderick Pearce (10)**
Brooklands School

## Winter

A beautiful view
Blue sprays coming down from it,
Looking like a herd.

Big raindrops dropping
Like planes falling from the sky,
Grey drops coming now.

The snow falls heavy now,
Over the hills and far away,
Like footballs coming.

The frost comes in winter,
The grass sticks up like swords now,
Don't come here anymore.

**Ronnie Raper (11)**
Brooklands School


## Night

The night rides in the dark,
No light, nothing, not a spark,
His are mines exploding with night
Like a deadly fight.

He runs through the night,
Throwing the balls of fright,
He sleeps at day
And he can see with x-ray.

His face is pale and white,
He uses all might,
To hide in the dark,
Behind a tree of bark.

**Ben Hunt (10)**
Brooklands School

# Reef Renga

Australia's reef
Tropical, colourful fish,
Bright coral just at night.

An aqua rainbow
Coral and anemones
Provide homes for fish.

Streaks of fin and scales
Beautiful multicoloured
Escaping the sharks.

Smooth and grey like lead
Hammerheads and great whites too
Thrashing their strange tails.

People coming down
From their homes to swim in the
Warm, dangerous sea.

Tidal waves so high
Look out, fish and people too
Plunging into froth.

The calm aftermath
Lives of creatures safe once more
Dangers gone for now.

**Phoebe Demeger (11)**
**Brooklands School**

## Night

Night comes smoothly
Along a dark street
He lights up faces
Whenever he speaks.

His dark hair blowing
His pale face light
Mysterious and creepy
He is a shadowy light.

He moves so silently
He makes no sound
On the quiet, peaceful
Healthy, grassy ground.

**Jack Humphrey (10)**
**Brooklands School**


## When I Grow Up

When I grow up
Will I be happy
And married?

Will I have
Lots of children
And will I be able to protect them?

Will my children
See the trouble
In the world?

If the world is violent
Will my children have children?

If my children have children,
Will I be a good grandad?

And if I'm a grandad
Will I tell my grandchildren
How my life in this world was?

**Jordan Blake Hancox (11)**
**Comber Grove Primary School**

## My Fears

I'm terrified they might split up
I get anxious so I take a sip from my cup
Oh I really hope they don't split up.

I think he's going to die
Every single day I cry and I cry
I think he's going to die.

Every day they ask me for money
If I don't they beat me up until morning
Every day they ask me for money.

I need money, a lot of it
I feel as if I'm at the bottom of a pit
I need money, a lot of it.

She kicks and punches me
Why can't she let me be?
She kicks and punches me.

She forgot about me and went with someone else
She betrayed me, but lives well
She forgot about me and went with someone else.

No one wants to be my friend, I'm all alone
I sit down at my table, in my empty little home,
No one wants to be my friend, I'm all alone.

Sometimes they forget I'm even here
They can't even see me, it's as if I'm part of the air,
Sometimes they forget I'm even here.

I know I'm going to fail
I'm going to be devastated when I receive my mail
I know I'm going to fail.

**Victoria Sylver (11)**
**Comber Grove Primary School**

# Will . . .

Will the grass always be green?
Will it grow and grow way up high?

Will the sea stay fresh and clean?
Will the sun still show in the blue sky?

Will the cows always graze?
Will the small plump hens
Cluck the way they used to?

Will we ever get lost in that high wall maze?
Will my family stay the way it was then
And me doing what I used to do?

Will schools stay the same?
Will bullying carry on,
Teachers trying their best?

Will I one day be taking the blame?
Will I be able to stand up strong
And stop all my crying and stress?

Will there be darkness?
No one there
And us children all alone?

Will there still be justice?
Will there still be someone who cares?
Still a place called home?

Will people still love?
Will I stay the same
Or will I fall apart?

**Georgia Reid-Hamilton (11)**
Comber Grove Primary School

# My Future

Will my mum
And dad break up
Altogether?

Or will they carry on
Being together forever?

Will they divorce
Or will they keep on going?

I think they'll divorce
Because of all
The arguments.

Will I feel left out
All the time?
I hate it.

Will my mum
And dad carry
On like this?

My sister
Always gets
Her own way.

Will she still
Get her own
Way after this day?

Will my future
Depend on
Me? Who can say?

**Tanya Villiers Read (10)**
Comber Grove Primary School

## My Fears

What would happen
If my father
Betrayed my mother?

Would my friend tell me
If she was getting bullied?

What would happen
If my parents got divorced?

How would I
Know when
The world is coming to an end?

Will I get
Debt when
I'm older?

Would my parents
Neglect me when
They had another baby?

Will I become
Homeless when
I am older?

If I'm bankrupt
Will I die
Of starvation?

When I die will
I go to Heaven
Or Hell?

**Alexandria Felix (11)**
Comber Grove Primary School

## My Fear

What will be
Left moving to a different
House every week?

What will be left
Once my parents die?
Nothing but my brother and I?

Once my parents are gone
There'll be nothing but
Their lovely two children!

If there was no dad,
Who would help me
With my homework?

If there was no mum
Who would play with
Me and make my life fun?

What would happen
If I failed the exams?
What would happen to me?

What if I made it in
My new school or would
I be bullied and decide to leave?

What if my parents die and
I was adopted
And abused by my new parents?

What if me and my brother got
Separated and we never saw each other again?

**Reiss McKenzie (11)**
**Comber Grove Primary School**

# My Future

What will happen
If my mum dies?
Will I be homeless?

If I die,
What will happen to me?
Will I be cremated?

Will I get
A good secondary school
To become something great?

Will I get
A job when I get older
To look after my family?

Will I get
A partner to then
Have a family with?

Will I get a good life
Or will it be full of loneliness?

Will I be rich
Or will I be
Poor with debts?

My destiny,
Will it be full of joy
Or will it be worthless?

Will I get a divorce
When I grow up
Or have a long lasting marriage?

**Cedric Nyankomango (11)**
Comber Grove Primary School

# What If My Cats . . .

What if my cats
Are starving to death
Or chewing upon my brand new bed?

What if my cats
Are hiding somewhere,
All alone with no one to help?

What if my cats
Are chasing a rat?
I hope it doesn't hide in my brand new hat

What if my cats
Are at the vet's
All scared and frightened and also upset?

What if my cats
Have climbed a tree
Way up high in the sky and can't get down?

What if my cats
Are alone and confused
Will people help or will they refuse?

What if my cats
Are left in the house
Scratching and miaowing whilst chasing a mouse?

What if my cats
Get left out in the rain,
Catching the flu and feeling the pain?

What will happen
To my precious cats?
Oh, what will happen to those on my mat?

**Cameo Montague-Raveneau (10)**
Comber Grove Primary School

# Fears In The Future

Will there be pollution in the air?
Will the oceans clean?

Will children's education improve and
Will they care?

What if animals escape from
London Zoo?

What if fairy tales come to life,
Won't that feel strange?

What if dinosaurs came back to life,
Will they still eat people?

What if people could fly instead
Or birds?

Will it snow?
Will children keep getting sick?

Suppose if all the food were eaten by snowmen?

What if aliens invaded the world,
Will people be scared?

What if all the good luck
Was used up, will we ever learn to lose?

**Priya Johura (10)**
Comber Grove Primary School

## My Future

What will be left here for me,
When I grow up?

Will parents stay exactly the same way
And never break up?

Will there still be houses
With beautiful roses,
Amongst white, picket fences?

Will friends remain together
And be like that forever and never depart?

Will people be ill and continue taking pills?
Will death still be near?

Will people stop dying,
Because it causes a lot of crying
And it hurts inside?

Will babies still be happy
And always wear a nappy
And sleep peacefully at night?

Will I get married
And never get worried
Because she'll be by my side?

Will I get a job
And a friend called Bob
And will we see each other every day?

**Adetunji Oduntan (10)**
**Comber Grove Primary School**

# The Future

Will there be anymore trees
To produce the beautiful leaves
And blow in the gentle breeze?

Will people still own pets,
For company and lots of joy?
When walking down the streets,
Will you see closed down vets?

Will there still be fish in the sea,
That swim around all day
Or will they have all died out
Five hundred years from today?

Will the jungles be bare,
Where animals live now?
Another question is will birds still fly in the air?

Will humans live in the sea,
Instead of living on land
Or will they just be on the edge,
Living on the sand?

In nearly every country,
Will there be starvation
So that you, your friends and family
Will have to change location?

Will there still be grass,
Growing on the ground
Or is a new type of plant likely to be found?

I wonder if in fifty years, life will ever be the same
Or if it's changed so much
I'll be saying 'What a shame!'

**Francesca Anderson (11)**
**Comber Grove Primary School**

# My Future

My future depends on me,
But I don't think it will,
Mum and Dad's divorcing!

They had fights,
That's not right,
They shout with all their might.

Will they go on forever?
I wish they never,
I want them to be together.

They don't say sorry,
I'd always worry,
I'd forget it and play with my toy lorry.

After the row,
Dad told Mum to go,
I hung my head low.

Then Stepmum came,
She gave me the blame,
Saying my welcoming is lame.

She brought me lots of toys
After she borne a boy,
I named him Roy.

I clambered into bed,
My face going red,
'Goodnight' she said.

Breakfast is berries!
Really wild cherries!
Roy is blowing raspberries!

I think that's my future
Don't know if I'm sure,
I hope it won't happen.

**Phuong Diep (10)**
**Comber Grove Primary School**

# Divorce

I'm feeling so sad,
I don't want it so bad,
Oh, please don't get a divorce!

When this is all over,
We will not argue ever,
Oh, please don't get a divorce!

What if I was good
And didn't nibble my hood
Oh, please don't get a divorce!

What if Dad gets a new family
And forgets about poor Emily
Oh, please don't get a divorce!

I don't care what they say
Dad's not going away
Oh, please don't get a divorce!

What if Mum gets a boyfriend
Who drives me round the bend
Oh, please don't get a divorce!

What about Sid?
He's only a little kid,
Oh, please don't get a divorce!

What about Jane?
I know she's a pain,
But, please don't get a divorce!

Look we love you all,
But our marriage has come to a fall,
So yes we're getting a divorce!

**Felicia Johnston (11)**
**Comber Grove Primary School**

# Rejection

Will everyone be rejected
From schools and jobs?

Will everyone just die,
Must we remain mortal?

If I move to a new house
Will I get bullied?

Will people make fun of me,
Just because I won't
Be able to see into the future?

What if parents
Just abandon their children?

What would happen if everyone in
The world was lonely?

What if none of us had any money,
To buy food and clothes?

Will people still be able
To breathe fresh air
Or will oxygen disappear?

**Carice Welch (10)**
**Comber Grove Primary School**

## What Will Happen In The Future?

What will be
Left here for me
When I grow up?

What will be left
In Africa if funds
Won't be made?

What will happen to
People if cancer
Keeps on striking?

What will happen
To children if they
Keep being abused?

What will happen
To animals if they
Keep being hunted?

What will happen to
People dying of starvation?

What will happen to children
If their parents abandon them?

What will happen if
There was no medicine
To cure illnesses?

What will happen
To the world
As we know it?

**Yasmin Chentouf (11)**
**Comber Grove Primary School**

# My Future

When I've grown up
Will people still care?
Will animals still be there?

Will they all be there?
Would you be able to hear the
Sweet sound of the birds?

Will there be no more
Spots or stripes?
Would there be nothing left?

Would all animals die out
Just as the dinosaurs
And the Dodo and mammoth did?

Would there be no more fish
Because the sea was
Polluted with rubbish and waste?

Will there be no cats or dogs,
Because of scientists doing
Animal testing on them?

Will elephants still be there?
Will the poachers have
Carried on or stopped?

Will there be
Any frogs left?
Cos they need clean air to breathe.

We wouldn't need
To ask these questions
If mankind didn't exist.

**Isabella Hernandez (11)**
**Comber Grove Primary School**

## My Fears

When it's raining, will flowers smile?
Will the grass dance and wave?
Will fields be happy?

Will trees die?
Will leaves fall?
Will birds have to move houses?

Will I still be a student?
Will I fall behind at tests?
Will I have many pleasures at school?

Will the sun change shape?
Will it still rise in the east?
Will it still descend in the west?

Will there be anymore pets?
Will animals still be kept in zoos?
Will all animals die out?

Will I see a goat?
Will I drink its milk again?
Will they be extinct?

The kettle is singing,
Smoke is running,
Is teatime coming?

Is there going to be rainbows?
Will the colours change?
Maybe there will be a colour missing?

If there isn't electricity, what will we use?
Will it always be dark at night?
At night, will there be no light?

**Kai Man Lee (10)**
**Comber Grove Primary School**

## My Life

Will I have a job to
Provide my family with?

Will there be people to talk
To in the future?

Will anything be left when I come here?

Will there be food left to eat
To keep people alive?

Will there be birds in
The morning to sing?

Will there be fresh air
In the morning to breathe?

My destiny is to keep trying
And never give up.

Will sunlight burn forests
That then burn down houses?

If I had a family
I'd treasure them with my life.

**Majid Kudsi (11)**
**Comber Grove Primary School**

## My Fear For The Future

I am afraid
That I will not
Have a wife.

I am afraid
That everything goes wrong
And I won't have a good life.

I am afraid
That no one will love me
And I will be all alone.

I am afraid
That I will be poor
And live on the street.

I am afraid
I will not be happy
And drink beer for the rest of my life.

I am afraid that
I will get sick
And have no money for medicine.

I am afraid that
I won't get a job
And live with my mum and dad all my life.

**George Wade (11)**
**Comber Grove Primary School**

# My Future

Will I live
A perfect
And successful life?

Will I get bullied
In my new secondary school?

Will I get a very good
And well-paid job?

What will happen to all
Living species?

Will people keep on dumping
Waste into the sea?

Will humans suffer too
Because of extinction, like animals?

Will my friends turn against each other?

Will I marry and intelligent and good-looking girl?

Will this world actually arrive at an end?

**Samuel Fagboyegun (11)**
Comber Grove Primary School

## The Magic Box
*(Based on 'Magic Box' by Kit Wright)*

I will put in my box . . .
A white tooth of a child
The cold snow from the North Pole
A brown tear of a young boy.

I will put in my box . . .
Some golden toys from a shop of treasure
The glittery blue moon that shines by night
A spirit of a newborn baby.

I will put in my box . . .
The shining yellow sun that shines by day
The bluest water you have ever seen
The first talking rainbow of many colours.

My box is fashioned with magic gold and silver
The corners are full of secrets
My box is made out of joy
I shall jump in my box to a nice
Sunny beach and swim in the sea.

**Treya Picking (7)**
**Comber Grove Primary School**

# The Magic Box
*(Based on 'Magic Box' by Kit Wright)*

I will put in the box . . .
For dreams to come true,
A tornado going right down to the sea,
A crab dancing with its friends.

I will put in the box . . .
A kitten with a star on its tail,
A big butterfly that came from spring,
A spring left turning pink and white.

I will put in the box . . .
The wind blowing on the summer sea,
A magic leaf that is shaped like a star,
A baby's first smile.

My box is fashioned invisible but not to me,
It is blue with magic glitter with yellow stars and wings,
Its hinges are made from stars.

I shall go to spring and on top of the sea
And go to another land and stay.

**Darnell Pluck (7)**
**Comber Grove Primary School**

## The Magic Box
*(Based on 'Magic Box' by Kit Wright)*

I will put in the box . . .
A picture of me and my mum,
A PlayStation with lots of games,
Henry shooting goals for Arsenal.

I will put in the box . . .
A glittery star rising in the sky,
Balloons bursting in the air,
Some toys dancing.

I will put in the box . . .
Flowers smelling of lemons next to your nose,
The green sun and animals dancing,
The wood breaking from the trees.

My box is fashioned from gold and grass,
With zigzags on the lid,
Its hinges are slices of lemons.

I shall surf in my box swimming all day
And I will play football in my box.

**Amran Sowe (7)**
**Comber Grove Primary School**

## Magic Box
*(Based on 'Magic Box' by Kit Wright)*

I will put in my box . . .
A petal from the first born rose in the spring,
A wish that I will stay in wonderland forever,
The first snowflake to fall on the ground.

I will put in my box . . .
A lily that had been floating in a pond,
A moon flower that shimmered in the sky light,
A heart that was once broken.

I will put in my box . . .
A star that sparkles in your hand at night,
A rainy day locked up in my dreams,
The first rocket to go to the moon.

My box is fashioned from golden stars and swirls,
Its hinges are golden shells and pebbles from the beach,
I shall sleep in my box forever and ever.

**Molly Petter (7)**
**Comber Grove Primary School**


## The Magic Box
*(Based on 'Magic Box' by Kit Wright)*

I will put in the box . . .
The glittery stars rising to the moon,
Flowers smelling of lemon next to your nose,
For everyone's dreams to come true.

I will put in the box . . .
Freddie Ljungberg shooting goals for Arsenal,
Pure white snow falling on your nose,
Party balloons falling in the sky like a rainbow.

My box is fashioned from stars from the sky
And icy snow.

I shall put my sister in my box.

**Chanyl Welch (7)**
**Comber Grove Primary School**

## The Magic Box
*(Based on 'Magic Box' by Kit Wright)*

I will put in my box . . .
The first bird that spoke to me,
The shimmer of the dark blue sea,
The smile from a parrot smiling at me.

I will put in my box . . .
The tear of a mermaid suddenly appearing,
The fresh air nothing but air,
The dark night watching me cry with fear.

I will put in the box . . .
The glittering star shining,
There, in a romantic place, love is falling apart,
There is a little kid singing *Twinkle Twinkle Little Star*.

I will put in the box . . .
The instant smell of seaweed,
The jumping dolphins saying, 'Hey! Look at me!'
The smell of the rising sea.

I will put in the box . . .
The song of the rising sun,
The bells of warning saying 'Run, just run.'
Babies rolling around for fun, fun, fun.

My box is fashioned with velvet blue
With a yellow ribbon around it with
Glitter stars surrounding it,
Its hinges are made from the yellowest piece
Of the moon.

I shall go to Heaven in my box gleaming like an angel,
I would go to Columbia to do the cha, cha, cha!
But the best place to be is in my soft, cosy bed.

**Emefa Ansah (8)**
**Comber Grove Primary School**

## The Magic Box
*(Based on 'Magic Box' by Kit Wright)*

I will put in the box . . .
The first snowball that drops on me,
The last rocket that reaches the moon,
A big star of candyfloss.

I will put in the box . . .
A golden ring that shines like my box,
A gold tooth like the sun,
A shell that sounds like the blue sea.

I will put in the box . . .
The sounds of the foggy wind blowing in my ear,
A sound of a beach ball about to pop,
A 1000 channel TV that springs out money.

My box is fashioned with blue pebbles on it like the ocean,
The lid is made out of shells. The edge is made from waves.

I shall eat in the box . . .
The candyfloss on a dark hill.

**Debbie Boyo (7)**
**Comber Grove Primary School**

## The Magic Box
*(Based on 'Magic Box' by Kit Wright)*

I will put in my box . . .
Shining stars in the clearest sky,
A small piece of a witch's finger,
A scaly tale of a dragon.

I will put in my box . . .
A million channel TV
That makes candyfloss
A golden star that touches my nose
A cold snowflake that tingles in the moonlight.

I will put in my box . . .
A small flower that touches my face,
A gold football that shoots goals,
A huge golden sun.

My box is fashioned with gold and silver,
The hinges are made of giant's toes.

I shall ride with a witch on her broomstick
And I shall race her to my house.

**Harry Locke (8)**
**Comber Grove Primary School**

# My Magic Box
*(Based on 'Magic Box' by Kit Wright)*

I will put in my box . . .
A horse that glides through the night
A small flower that talks to you when you're sad
A secret door that I can go in.

I will put in my box . . .
Drama people and they will dance all night
Sweets that entertain you
A flower that pops up and cuddles you.

I will put in my box . . .
The star that gives you a wish
A witch that gives you a ride and
Brings you home safely.

My box is made out of winter snow
That does not know where it's going.

In my box we shall have a festival every night
Nobody can see it except for me,
I shall go to the beach in my box and
Eat fruit and play in the water,
While the sun goes down.

**Rebecca Pritchard (7)**
**Comber Grove Primary School**

## My Magic Box
*(Based on 'Magic Box' by Kit Wright)*

I will put in the box . . .
The starlight of Christmas
The best taste of pancakes,
A silver star that shines in the moonlight.

I will put in the box . . .
A hairbrush with a gleaming ocean handle,
Glass sweets that came all the way from Venice
A very colourful bird that lives in a big cage.

I will put in the box . . .
The delicious smell of fish and chips,
The best ever smell of marshmallows in hot chocolate
The touch of gooey dough.

My box is fashioned with a yellow ribbon around the top
I shall jump on my bed inside my box
And break all the springs!

**Kit Pearson (7)**
**Comber Grove Primary School**


## The Magic Box
*(Based on 'Magic Box' by Kit Wright)*

I will put in the box . . .
The glittery stars rising to the moon,
Flowers smelling of lemon next to your nose,
For everyone's dreams to come true.

I will put in the box . . .
Freddie Ljungberg shooting goals for Arsenal,
Pure white snow falling on your nose,
Party balloons floating to the sky like a rainbow.

My box is fashioned from gold and
Is wooden and cannot break even a bit,
I shall swim around my box looking at it.

**Liam Walter (8)**
**Comber Grove Primary School**

# The Magic Box
*(Based on 'Magic Box' by Kit Wright)*

I will put in my box . . .
A sparkly star
The shine from glittering gold
A magical bell that lights up your hand.

I will put in my box . . .
A prickly hedgehog
A colourful flying bird
A shivery butterfly.

I will put in my box . . .
Melting ice
The first aeroplane
And the waving sea.

I will put in my box . . .
A giant dinosaur that lays bird eggs
A sharp tooth from the monster
And a tiny brown mouse.

My box is fashioned with gleaming stars and moons
The corners are made from golden metals,
There is a ribbon on top.

I shall swim in the cold wavy sea in my box and
Play on the golden sandy beach.

**Anwaar Ali (7)**
**Comber Grove Primary School**

## My Magic Box
*(Based on 'Magic Box' by Kit Wright)*

I will put in the box . . .
A shall which sounds like the sea,
A tropical fish the colour of the rainbow.

I will put in the box . . .
God in my locket
With a picture of my family,
Messages for friends and family
And wishes for a pet.

I will put in the box . . .
A television with Sky on it,
A CD player safe to play with my friends,
My secrets that no one has told.

My box is fashioned with sequins,
Ice and steal,
With pom-poms on the lid,
Its hinges are made out of stars.

I shall sing in my box
On the fluffiest cloud, the colour of snow.

**Lêvyne Haughton (8)**
**Comber Grove Primary School**

# The Magic Box
*(Based on 'Magic Box' by Kit Wright)*

I will put in my box . . .
A soft calm breeze brushing over me,
Shooting stars flying through the quiet sky
And the moon coming to me.

I will put in my box . . .
A pig that flies through the air
With a cloak swishing through the trees,
A snowman flying through the soft sky.

I will put in my box . . .
A monster that is a vegetarian,
A cow that jumps over the moon,
With a cloak on that talks.

My box is fashioned from snow with stars
The lid is made from glass
Its hinges are made from half a moon.

I shall fly in my box
And drink water that turns into red wine.

**Adam Bouhlouba (8)**
**Comber Grove Primary School**

## The Magic Box
*(Based on 'Magic Box' by Kit Wright)*

I will put in my box . . .
A picture of my family who I love
The glittery stars that shine in the night
A TV that comes out with really shiny sweets.

I will put in my box . . .
The soft, smooth clouds that light up
A cowboy riding on a white glittery horse
My teddy that's smooth and cuddly.

I will put in my box . . .
The fresh flowers that are so bright and cold
Some treasure and a gold necklace
That has a picture of me in when I was a baby.

My box is fashioned in swirls that
Swish in the night,
A wish that wishes me a dream
And a starry diamond ruby.

I shall sleep in my box and
Have the best dream ever.

**Amber Hawgood (7)**
**Comber Grove Primary School**

## The Magic Box
*(Based on 'Magic Box' by Kit Wright)*

I will put in the box . . .
The waves crashing in the ocean
People singing for joy
Mermaids singing happily.

I will put in the box . . .
Children playing peacefully
Seagulls flying across the ocean
Snakes hissing on the ground.

I will put in the box . . .
A dolphin swimming in the sea
Wolves howling as loud as they can
Bees buzzing their way to their beehive.

My box is fashioned from gold stars
And lots of silver,
It's got a spotty leather lid
Its hinges are made out of leather strings.

I shall skateboard on my box
Sail the seven seas
And play PlayStation quietly.

**Ishmael Atterh (7)**
**Comber Grove Primary School**

# The Magic Box
*(Based on 'Magic Box' by Kit Wright)*

I will put in the box . . .
A brick from St Paul's
The first picture of gran that I ever saw
A speck of my curled black hair.

I will put in my box . . .
The loud crashing sound of the sea
A sweet maker that never finishes
A gold and silver tower of light.

I will put in my box . . .
My mum's first kiss
My wonderful secret diary
My nana's lovely sweet smell.

I will put in my box . . .
A night full of stars
Raindrops on roses
The nice taste of a chocolate milkshake.

My box is fashioned with shiny silk
And lovely jelly sweets that never go away.

I shall sunbathe on my box
Swim with dolphins and make up songs
Whilst dreaming of a cheesy Greek salad.

**Amber Maurice (8)**
**Comber Grove Primary School**

# The Magic Box
*(Based on 'Magic Box' by Kit Wright)*

I will put in my box . . .
Lightning from a rainy night
The burning bush of an apple tree
The sound of waves swishing to and fro.

I will put in my box . . .
A girl on the waves of a song,
Dancing in a ballerina dress
A cup of gold from a palace
A table of dreams.

I will put in my box . . .
A crown covered in jewels
That shine like the sun
A case of a locket as beautiful as gold.

My box is fashioned from safari and
Shells from the sea
My dreams of the yellow sun
The twinkle of a star.

I shall sleep in my box
In a boat on the great big sea.

**Rachel Sanguinetti (7)**
**Comber Grove Primary School**

## My Magic Box
*(Based on 'Magic Box' by Kit Wright)*

I will put in my box . . .
A gleaming necklace
Silver jewels gleaming in the dark blue sky
The sounds of a bird's hum.

I will put in my box . . .
The shimmer of the deep blue sea
Pearls like you have never seen before
Light silver lipstick shining in the dark night sky.

I will put in my box . . .
Sweet strawberries
Shiny pink stars
And a dolphin's soft voice.

My box is fashioned with gold and silver
And diamonds like a starry night.

I shall dance in my box
I shall dance on the blue tip of an icicle.

**Ammarah Hamilton (8)**
**Comber Grove Primary School**

# My Fears

People who used to
Live happily
Will it always last?

The people who lived
Did they have
My fears?

Will the couple
Who were married
Last forever?

Will the people who
Starve ever have
Food to eat?

Will people stop
Destroying
This world?

What about the animals?

Will they still be as happy as they look now?
Will they run around as though they didn't
Have a care in the world?

Will the happiness
Last forever?

When I grow,
Will everything be gone?

When will the illness stop?

**Omolade Agoro (11)**
Comber Grove Primary School

# The Magic Box
*(Based on 'Magic Box' by Kit Wright)*

I will put in my box . . .

The floor moving out and in the box
A big flower covering the world
The sand rushing through my fingers.

I will put in my box . . .

The green sun and animals dancing
Frogs yellow and blue and red
Dogs climbing trees.

I will put in my box . . .

Toys that talk and dance
The wind pushing through my hair
Cows that walk on two legs.

My box is fashioned red and yellow stripes
It is made from plastic silver and gold
Its hinges are tiger claws.

I shall sit on the sun in my box
It is the colour of a bright sunny lemon.

**Emeka Orazulume (8)**
**Comber Grove Primary School**

## The Magic Box
*(Based on 'Magic Box' by Kit Wright)*

I will put in my box . . .
The glittery stars rising
To the moon,
Flowers smelling of
Lemon next to your nose,
For everyone's dreams to come true.

I will put in the box . . .
Freddie Ljungberg
Shooting goals for Arsenal,
Pure white snow falling
From the sky on your nose,
Party balloons floating in
The air like a rainbow.

My box is fashioned with gold
And patterns of silver.

**Devante Rodney-Francis (8)**
**Comber Grove Primary School**


## The Magic Box
*(Based on 'Magic Box' by Kit Wright)*

I will put in my box . . .
The spectacular roar when
Chelsea score and
Win The Premiership,
I will put in my box
The six slippery snakes
As a rope ladder and vines,
I will put in my box the swish of a broom
As I walk across the horizon.

**Freddie Price (9)**
**Dulverton Primary School**

## War Poem

Houses burning brightly,
Loved ones lost,
Fire bullets being shot,
Four people down,
One remaining.

Houses burning brightly,
Loved ones lost,
Bullets whistling
Through the air,
One man shot down,
Sweet death, sweet revenge.

Blood spread all over the battlefield,
People lying on the floor,
Eventually turning into maggots,
Left ones remaining from the war.

People dying,
People crying,
Their relatives dead
In the battlefield.

**Oliver Denyer (10)**
**Dulverton Primary School**


## Pollution

Fish closer to family
One wandering off
To touch the deep
Instantly murdered
Goldfish frozen
On steel ice
Oil slick rushes in
Like a waterfall
Fish die.

**Mollie Selfe (9)**
**Dulverton Primary School**

## Poisoned River

Running,
Sliding,
Gliding, into the rapids
Down to the waterfall
Flowing like a bird in the air
Gushing into toxic poison
All that is good is now bad
Fishes struggling like a bug being
Squashed
Not clean, just sludge
All that once lived is now poisoned.

**Thomas Duncumb (9)**
**Dulverton Primary School**


## Partridge

Its fine feathers
Its perfect song
Wishes you a merry Christmas
And a happy new year.

It sits in a pear tree
And waits patiently to see
If it will be
Number one
For Christmas.

**Michael Burton (9)**
**Dulverton Primary School**

## War Hero

In the battlefields
The hero stands
In the protection
Of imaginary body armour
Shooting
A bullet comes
A bullet goes
As people get shot down
Blood smears uniforms
Blood on the ground
The hero still stands.

**Sam Briggs (9)**
**Dulverton Primary School**


## Friends

Friends are the best,
Friends are the future,
Open your eyes, take a look,
See what friends can do,
They can make you laugh,
Help you through things,
Give you advice
So if you want a friend like this,
Just make sure you look around and see.

**Yeliz Mustafa (10)**
**Dulverton Primary School**

# River

Crystal clear
Almost like glass
Glittering like a thousand diamonds
Fresh, cool water
Trickling over little stones and pebbles
Seeping through rocks and grass
Running down a mountain
Clean
Reaching for the climax

Gradually growing bigger and *bigger* and *bigger*
Finally reaching denouement
Flowing gently
Now about three times the size
But, still getting larger
Swooping in and out of huge rocks and forests of vines
Never stopping for a break
Just keeps going on
Five feet deep
Eight feet wide
Passers-by dazzled, hypnotised
Not for long
Like an army of bees
Black oozing, gooey oil
Starts seeping into the
Sky-blue, crystal clear, even soft river
Like a human heart
It stops beating with a touch of damage
This human heart has stopped
It's dead.
Moving slowly
Not fresh anymore
Chocolate pigment
Foul-smelling, a disgrace to everyone
Blaming the bleached river
All they have to blame is
Themselves.

**Bryony Bonner (9)**
**Dulverton Primary School**

## River

Running river
Colours shimmering
Rushing fast with its fins
Meandering swiftly round like a kingfisher
Never stopping, always going
Like a wind it sweeps by
Going to one place
But stopped on its way
By a slithery snake
*Oil*
Sweeping along, it spreads
Into the swirling rapids
Slaying the fish like gladiators
Slaughtering the river.

**Kira Thorne-Smith (9)**
**Dulverton Primary School**


## Chocolate Harvest

The Galaxy melts in my hands
All creamy and gooey
So silky and messy
So yummy and enchanting
A gorgeous, rich, scented smell
With a lovely taste of harvest.

**Ellie Custy (9)**
**Dulverton Primary School**

## Harvest

Autumn comes
Seeping through a hole in summer
Like blood from a cut
The farmers come to harvest their food
Before Winter strikes
Luscious apples fall from the green trees
Giant juicy cherries are waiting to be plucked
Golden crops glow with pride in the gorgeous sunshine
The leaves fall off the trees leaving them bare
The plants die
Death guides Winter on its journey
To make Autumn flee.

**Joseph Coughlin (9)**
**Dulverton Primary School**

## Glistening River

Glistening like an icicle
flying like a golden eagle
fish spring up and down
flowers all around
forced back like a Roman army
fish lying on the ground
like a battlefield of dead people.

**Jack Ward (10)**
**Dulverton Primary School**

## The Worst Valentine

Roses are red, violets are blue
You make me tingle when I think of you
For your sleek black hair
And your big puppy dog eyes
But when I look into them
I realise
That it's just some kind of disguise
You don't really love me, you won't socialise
So I'd never marry a person like you
Because you're a liar
And a faker too.

**Charlotte Avis (9)**
**Dulverton Primary School**


## Christmas Eve

Christmas Eve
Church bells ring
Santa is coming,
Carols at your door
Children sing galore
Santa is coming,
Morning comes
Children open their presents
Christmas Eve,
Gone
Looking forward to next year.

**Alise Cotton (9)**
**Dulverton Primary School**

## Disappearing

You make it
You celebrate it
The melted snow drifts
Down my cheek
A lost tear
A missing poster
The happiness
The joy
The sadness
The sorrow
It's gone, all gone
Goodbye snowman.

**Ellie Barnfield (9)**
**Dulverton Primary School**


## River

The river glides through the country,
As clean as a whistle,
Later fertilisers rain over the river,
Terminating her slippery slimy children,
However, she smoothly carries on.
Later on, oil seeps slyly from a ship,
Murdering her white squawking hats.

**James Roberts (9)**
**Dulverton Primary School**

# River

A year earlier
She was spotless
Polished and crystalline
She could glide
Up and down
Nothing stopping her
Discharged
She could go anywhere
But a year later
She slowed
Didn't flow
Filthy
Dead
Pollution filled her
Life up
And away
She went.

**Joanna Sheldon (9)**
Dulverton Primary School

# River

The sunlight smashing the water into
Finely-cut segments of diamonds
Creating blinding rays of light.
Impaling everything in its path
Crushing rocks, woodland, granite
Like a bulldozer.
The river is fed by the source
In the mountains
But it ends up
At the sea.

**Alex Wade (10)**
Dulverton Primary School

## My Magic Box
*(Based on 'Magic Box' by Kit Wright)*

I will put in my box . . .
Fire as red as a Chinese dragon's heart,
The first snowflake as white as a baby's tooth.
I will put in my box . . .
A statue who dreams that he could move,
A white horse as white as the first winter snow.
I will put in my box . . .
Six stripy snakes of the hot Australia.
I will put in my box . . .
The last word of Jesus,
The first word Noah said.

**Graham Frith (10)**
**Dulverton Primary School**


## War

Bang! One down,
Bang! Another man down,
Lives lost to save us,
Smoke choking soldiers,
Every second a life lost,
Tears falling from every soldier,
As their loves pray they're not dead,
Bullets whistle through the air,
Explosions getting closer and closer.
Boom! Boom!
Silence strikes the air.

**James Thomas (9)**
**Dulverton Primary School**

## A River Poem

A river's beginning is where the coldest winds blow,
Where there are the highest coolest mountains,
Melting trickles of snow change into a pure blue river,
It flows gently through the countryside,
Meandering like a snake wriggling in the grass,
The sun making the river sparkle
Like pearls glimmering on the sea floor,
The river is a cool blue colour,
Changing as it moves,
Brushing over banks,
Rushing left and right,
Looking for its destiny,
The sea, running down waterfalls,
Waiting to reach where it belongs,
Dashing in and out of rocks and stones,
Finally reaching the sea,
The deep blue sea.

**Sarah Wood (10)**
**Dulverton Primary School**


## Water

Water running down a mountain
Bumping on rocks on a journey
To the big sea
As it speeds to its target
Splashing and sploshing still on a
Ferocious journey to its destiny
The wide ocean, on it goes
Faster and faster, finally it
Gets there and enjoys its pure
Water, it spreads all around, the
Sea gets bigger, the journey is over.

**Joe Squires (9)**
**Dulverton Primary School**

# In a River

Little breathing bubbles
discovered beneath a rock,
schools of fish swim by
with little silver rudd,
lots of tiny twisters
conjuring up in the
water like big black
holes sucking up
everything in its path,
with its meander
crashing against
the sides of rocks
and chipping the edges
into harmless corners.

**Georgina Oram (10)**
Dulverton Primary School

# Best Friends

B est friends should stick together
E verlasting friendship
S ian, Mary, Amy, Yeliz
T ogether forever.

F riendship that lasts through
R ough times and good
I n and out of clubs together
E verlasting friendship
N o one can break us up
D iving in pools together
S ian, Mary, Amy and Yeliz.

**Sian Qureshi (10)**
Dulverton Primary School

## Fairies

Fairies, pixies, goblins too
I believe, but do you?
Down in the woods you may see
Dancing fairies under a tree.
There they sing their mysterious songs,
Oh, I wish I could belong
To their world of magic and calm.
There I know I would come to no harm,
If you want to come and see
You are welcome to come along with me
To experience this wonderful sight,
It is truly a delight.
But to see the fairies dance
You must first believe, to stand a chance.
Fairies, pixies, goblins too,
I believe, but do you?

**Sophie Moulder (10)**
**Dulverton Primary School**

## The War

Men trying to fight for our country,
*Bang, bang*, two shots, two men down.
Soldiers choking from the smoke,
Young children being made to fight.
Wives traumatised because their husbands are dead,
Flames burning houses.
Life lost from young children,
Innocent people dying.

**Harrison Dark (9)**
**Dulverton Primary School**

## Tiger

I like the tiger,
But sometimes I fear the tiger,
Day is when it sleeps,
But night is when it leaps,
It eats different meats,
When it runs,
Fast is how its heart beats,
Sometimes it bounces,
Sometimes it pounces,
If you put up a fight,
You will get a bite,
If you don't leave him alone,
You will be his bone,
Why does it live in the trees?
Does it hurt when it gets stung by bees?
Does it like killing people?
Does it like eating people?
I'm not sure I like the tiger.

**Rosie Gillham (8)**
**Dulverton Primary School**

## Death

Death is a horrid thing
travelling, killing
Death has no friends
no family
just the people he kills.

**Joe Brown (10)**
**Dulverton Primary School**

## Music

The quavers sit humming
A soft melodious tune.
The crotchets rest
Side by side.
Along the staves, stretching bars.
The rhythmic sound of the semi-breve
Flows through the atmosphere.
The noise of the music floats
Through the air,
Unending,
Until the flicking pages fall together,
Enclosing the notes,
For another musical day.

**Eleanor Minney (11)**
**Dulverton Primary School**


## What Am I?

Grabbing the sand
rippling your feet
destroying castles
venturing further
gathering junk
scaring youngsters.

What am I?

**Mark Blaylock (10)**
**Dulverton Primary School**

## The Bathroom

'Quickly! No one's here.'
The light switch pulls itself on,
To start the fun!
The groans of rough towels,
And the hiss of the shower,
The toothpaste tube's blood
Bubbles with excitement

*Midnight strikes*

Loo roll jumps up and down,
While the pipes gurgle with laughter,
Deodorants hop back towards the shelf,
The sink clears its throat
Ready for any liquid for him to drink.
Silence falls
As footsteps are heard
Coming up the stairs.

**James Dix (10)**
Dulverton Primary School


## The River

The river whistles in the storm like the wind on a rainy day.
The river bends like a winding snake on the sand in the desert.
It meanders over the hills,
and sounds like a tap running loudly.
The sun changes the river's colour,
when it catches it, it looks like
thousands of segments of diamonds on the river's sandy bed.
It flows gently through the lake and the river ends up
on the wide, clear ocean.

**Nicola Gallagher (9)**
Dulverton Primary School

## Cat

Cute cat, sly cat, sleeping in the night cat,
Is it quick, is it slow?
Does it play all night in the snow?
Cute and cuddly, swift and smooth,
A cute cuddly kitten just for you,
Feed it well, brush it well,
And it will love you just as well.

**Emily Bruce (8)**
**Dulverton Primary School**


## Kittens

Kitten curls up cosy,
Soft furry, purr purr,
Sit by the fire, all hot and warm,
Falls asleep in her basket,
Curls up by the fire,
All happy and joyful in the morning.

**Lucy Carroll (10)**
**Dulverton Primary School**


## Snowflake

Flossy white . . .
Cold as night.
Sparkling on the ground,
Flashing like a star,
That's what you are . . .
Snowflake.

**Joe Sullivan (10)**
**Dulverton Primary School**

## Morning

I wake up to the sound of the Amazon birdsong

I stretch like a lazy lion

Padding to the bathroom the floorboards creak like monkeys swinging through the vines

I change my clothes like a chameleon

My belly roars like a tiger, breakfast is ready and I eat slowly like a gorilla enjoys fruit from the tree

My pack of friends have arrived - it's time to leave my nesting ground and explore the jungle

I'm ready to begin another adventurous day.

**Jake Gill (11)**
**Dulverton Primary School**


## The Garden

The grand oak tree sways in the small breeze,
The flowers whisper silently to each other
As they settle down to sleep.
The moon is covered by a thick mist,
Animals scamper back to their homes,
Fireflies flutter about the garden
As midnight approaches.

**Daniel Jenkins (10)**
**Dulverton Primary School**

## The New Baby

Baby got a rattle,
Baby got a ball,
Baby got a blanket,
I got nothing at all!

Baby got attention,
Baby got loved,
Baby got cuddles,
I got shoved!

Baby goes to bed now
straight after tea.

I get to stay up later
and watch TV!

**Laura Curwood (11)**
**Dulverton Primary School**


## Black Horse

I see his black hooves trotting down
The lane as his head raises and lowers
Every time his hooves pound on the
Pebbles that are scattered all over the
Dusty old lane, his rider holding the
Short but strong rope that is tied to the
Collar that is strapped to his neck.
His name is Sparrow, Black Sparrow.

**Oliver Potter (10)**
**Dulverton Primary School**

## The Woods

It's a crisp Sunday morning
In the middle of winter
It's a walk in the woods
With my companion Splinter.

We can see the horses
We can hear the birds
As we cross over the bridge
We see cattle in herds.

The trees are naked
The tips of plants appear
Spring is approaching
Bringing new baby deer.

**Edward Healy  (11)**
**Dulverton Primary School**


## Max

I will never be able to play with him again,
I will never be able to stroke him again,
I loved him like no other pet.
I was nervous sitting at the vet's waiting,
Waiting, waiting, waiting.
Until out comes no Max.
No Max to play with, no Max to stroke.
Max, Max, Max.
All I could think of is him
Every day and every night.

**Sarah Banks  (10)**
**Foxfield School**

## Untitled

'Who is on the phone, Mother?'
I'm so cold.
'Who is knocking at the door, Mother?
Is it Lulu, Mother?'

'What has happened to Lulu, Mother?
Where is she?'
I'm so alone,
I don't know what to do.

I heard Lulu's voice,
But it sounded like a bird,
'Mother, is it Lulu?'
'Yes it is!'

'Lulu, how are you?'
She took a bow,
We gave her a clap,
She ran upstairs.

**Tanyia Beg**
Foxfield School

## My Long-Lost Lover And I

My lover,
My one true lover,
She is gone,
She is gone for good, for I love her very deeply and now she is gone,
My heart is broken, my tears gone cold for my long-lost lover and I.
My girl,
My girl is more precious than the crown jewels,
My girl is more precious than the throne of England,
She was the most beautiful girl around town,
And the most beautiful also in my heart.

**Ayodeji Akintinmehin (9)**
Foxfield School

## Untitled

I went to her friend's house,
I asked her friend for her,
her friend shrugged her shoulders
and replied, 'Shoo!'

'There's someone at the door, Mother,
there's someone at the door,
should I have a look, Mother,
please, just once?'

'Stop crying, Mother, you're making me upset,
stop trying to hide your face,
I can see the tears drop,
what is the case?'

'I heard the doorbell ring, Mother,
I heard the doorbell ring.'
I went to open it,
it was Lulu coming.

**Ankita Dilesh**
**Foxfield School**


## Knowing Bess

Knowing Bess is my life
Knowing she is my soul
Knowing she is my gun
Knowing she is my love

Knowing she is my meaning to live
Knowing she is my queen
Knowing she was all I had
Knowing she was my heart

Knowing she is my goddess
Knowing she has left my heart
Knowing she has left my life
Knowing that I will not be able to share
my dreams with her again.

**Connor Whitworth (9)**
**Foxfield School**

## What Happened To Lulu?

'What has happened to Lulu?
Why don't you tell me, Mother?
Why can't you tell me?
Why don't you bother?'

I tried to look everywhere
There's no sign
There's no one to help
I don't know if she's fine.

'I'm scared, Mother
I'll try to look again
We're all alone
I don't want to be in pain.

'Why can't you get any help, Mother?
Mother, I heard the doorbell ring.'
I went to answer it
It was Lulu coming in.

**Ruksana Begum (10)**
**Foxfield School**


## The biggest Loss Of My Life

Losing a loved one is like having a part of your heart
Being taken away forever, forever, forever
Losing a loved one is like having a part of your heart
Being taken away forever

When a loved one gets taken away your emotions go mad
When a loved one gets taken away your heart gets
Permanently damaged

You wish that they'll come back, when they don't
Your hopes get shattered
Your hopes prove useless
But keep your head up.

**Mohammad Mirza (10)**
**Foxfield School**

# What Happened To Lulu?

'What makes your tears come down, Mother?'
I walked to Lulu's best friend's house,
I walked back home and I went upstairs,
And saw Lulu's pet mouse.

'Do you know where Lulu went, Mother?'
But it is calm,
And I feel so lonely without her,
I can also hear Lulu's clock alarm.

'I need a hug, I can't forget her, Mother,
Can I go and find Lulu?'
I will find her one day,
But I will find a clue.

'I want Lulu back, Mother.'
But I'm still sad,
Will she come back?
I can even get mad.

'I can hear someone upstairs, Mother,
Is it Lulu? It can't be.'
'Yes, it is,
Did you miss me?'

**Annabelle Vuong (9)**
Foxfield School

## Untitled

My love is breaking
against me and the highwayman.
*How am I going to warn him?*
*Who is going to know?*

*I've got a good idea*
*but am I brave enough?*
*I think I am*
*but am I doing the right thing?*

I start to hear the sounds,
click, clack, clickity, clack.
I push down the trigger
and there and then . . .

I will always
remember him upon my heart,
and in the corner of my black eye
and never to forget him.

And I will never forget
that last tear in my eye,
and hopefully our spirit of
love will carry on.

**Kelsey Ashley (10)**
**Foxfield School**


## Feelings Of The Blitz

The air raid siren's just gone off,
    I'm scared, terrified and unhappy.
I want to move away from the bombs,
    Oh, no! I've forgotten my teddy-bear.
Oh, wait! It's over there.
    'Mum, can we go back inside?
Where's the house?'
    Where could it be?
        Has it been bombed?
Yes!

**Latisha Francis-Rose (11)**
**Heavers Farm Primary School**

## Feelings Of The Blitz

Air raids going off everywhere,
As I sit inside and stare.
Oh no! Here they come,
Bombing us as we run.
There's not enough food to go around,
So we grow our own food from the ground.
The bombing's getting worse, it really is,
They don't even care they made the Blitz.
We want to run although we can't,
They won't stop bombing, they shan't, they shan't.
The Germans, you see, they want to kill me,
I tried to run but they'll always find me,
I've given up running now.
They keep killing, keep killing, keep killing.

**Kieron Nurse (10)**
**Heavers Farm Primary School**


## So Scared

Sorrowful,
Frightened, fearful,
Just so scared.
Betrayed by my family,
Abandoned in the big sea,
Nobody will ever come for me!
I am as empty as a box.
The boat rocks like a baby!
I am sick of the depths of the sea
Troubled, terrified,
Of the deep, deep sea!

**Holly Eastoe (10)**
**Heavers Farm Primary School**

## My School

I am going to tell you
A bit about my school.
It is called Heavers Farm,
And it is really cool.

Our classes are named after colours,
At the moment I'm in green.
In yellow, indigo, crimson and purple
I have also been.

I haven't forgotten amber,
The teacher was just great.
I loved all the lessons
And never wanted to be late.

I'm going to tell you a little bit more
About the fun things that we do.
There's football, cricket and the choir,
I play the violin too.

But the fun doesn't end there
Because of all the places we see.
Museums, parks and London Zoo,
The science trip was best for me.

So now my tale is at the end,
I hope you enjoyed my say.
The hard work, but also the fun
I have during my school day.

**Stevie-Jane Watson (10)**
**Heavers Farm Primary School**


## Pets

I like guinea pigs because they're soft and sweet.
I like hamsters because they have got cute feet.
I like cats because they are funny.
Most of all, I love my bunny!

**Joanne Boyd (10)**
**Heavers Farm Primary School**

# Family

Brothers and sisters,
Mum and Dad.
They're my best friends,
closest friends,
that I will ever have.

They care for me,
look after me,
when I'm feeling down.
When I need something,
they are always around.

They sometimes give me treats,
on Easter and my birthday,
they are always kind,
and they don't mind,
if I get my own way!

**Johannah Fening (10)**
**Heavers Farm Primary School**


# A Spooky Night

It was all dark across the town
Ghosts and ghouls were all about
Children fast asleep in their beds
Whilst the immortal world was creating horror
The clock struck twelve and the human world awoke
To start another day, so all evil went away.

**Samuel Derek Willis (9)**
**Heavers Farm Primary School**

## The Evacuated Girl

My mum told me a terrible thing,
I was to leave next morning.
The next morning I packed my bags,
As my mother gave me all the tags.
As I watched my mum speed by,
I couldn't help myself but cry.
In the train there was a horrible girl,
Whose name just happened to be Amanda Pearl.
As I clung onto my favourite ted,
The house was there and this is what I said:
'This home is dark and gloomy,
It's making me feel very lonely.'
My host family treat me very bad,
Sometimes it makes me very mad.
I'm always the one to blame,
By that awful boy called Wayne.
I wish my mum would come and get me,
Because of this horrible host family.
Wayne thinks he's so much smarter,
But I think he's as dumb as garters.
As I wrote my letter
I felt a little better.
Oh Mum please try and get me!

**Zoe Charlesworth (11)**
**Heavers Farm Primary School**


## The Weekend

W eekend is on Saturday and Sunday,
E veryone has a wonderful time,
E verybody rest and play,
K eep it up, go, go, go,
E veryone likes a lay-in,
N ot an early start,
D o the right thing and enjoy it while it lasts.

**Stephanie Allen (10)**
**Heavers Farm Primary School**

## Feelings Of An Evacuee

    Miserable, miserable me,

Oh no here they come
Feeling like I want to run

    Miserable, miserable me,

Oh Mum
What have you done?

    Miserable, miserable me,

Dark house, dull room
Turn a different way, doom, doom, doom,

Miserable, miserable me,

Feeling scared,
Very unhappy, smelling like a sour nappy,
Wanting to just run away,
Never took a bath today.

Miserable, miserable me,

Oh Mum what have you done?
I just want to run, run away
Never return
Is she really concerned?

Miserable, miserable me.

**Ebbony Samuda (10)**
Heavers Farm Primary School


## Remember

Remember when I hugged you
Remember when I was ill
Remember all the times we spent together and always will.
Remember when we laughed
Remember when I cried and you were always there for me.
Now you're gone you're still in my heart
My memory and I will never part.

**Rebecca Allen & Georgina Thomas (10)**
Heavers Farm Primary School

## Happy Cabin Boy

I feel so nervous
I think my parents did it on purpose
Fantastic and free
Sailing the sea.

We sailed the sea
While I felt unhappy
I do too much work each day
Never enough time to run and play
I feel so sad
I feel so bad.

I miss Mum when she does that hum
She always said to me
Don't be rude to Dad or Lee.

**Ricky Dunn (10)**
**Heavers Farm Primary School**


## The Beach

T umbling waves swishing and whooshing,
H ordes of people gathering around,
E mpty cars just sitting waiting.

B rollies up as the sun shines down,
E ighty deckchairs have all been used,
A unties and uncles still waiting in the queue,
C hildren playing with buckets and sand,
H appiness is all you can see, as nothing is like a great day
                  at the beach.

**Jenny Matthews (9)**
**Heavers Farm Primary School**

## Sold For Money!

Abandoned!
All alone in the middle of the sea.
Betrayed
By my dear own family!
Sold for money!
Confused!
*Why have they done this to me?*
Unloved
By the people I care about!
Sold for money!
How exciting!
Sensational, spectacular, how the sea moves,
Blessed, blissful, by the power of the sea.
How exciting!
I am lucky, I am proud
To be on the big blue sea.
How exciting!

**Rebecca Allen (11)**
**Heavers Farm Primary School**


## Why?

I look up at the sky and I think how or why
Is the sky so high?
Or why is it blue not green
Or even tangerine?
All this thinking gets me wishing
I could be up there floating in the air,
Flying with the planes, little birds and bees,
I'd love to do that, please, please, oh please!

**Jordan Williams (10)**
**Heavers Farm Primary School**

## Friendship

Friendship is good
friendship is bad
sometimes it makes
you very sad.

People lie, people cry
some day it will
pass you by!

So try and keep your
friendships.

**Rea Lilliard (10)**
Heavers Farm Primary School


## I'm A Cabin Girl!

C alm is the sea,
A bsurd is the creature,
B allistic is me!
I ll is my friend,
N ew is my job.

G reat it is at sea,
I mage is what the monster was,
R unning is my good,
L ove is me and my family.

**Chrissie Kiby (11)**
Heavers Farm Primary School

## Unhappy Cabin Boy

I'm sick of the big wide sea
I want to see land with nature's glee
I'm really scared of the big waves
I wish I could be really brave
And so I wish I was at home
Snug as snug could be.

I'm angry, scared and annoyed
Did my parents love me?
I am terrified that we might be heading
Towards a sea monster or a desert island
I am confused
And feel really used.

**Sophie Wyllie (11)**
Heavers Farm Primary School


## Unhappy

I am very lonely and frightened
And sad not to see you
I am unhappy without you
It is very cold near the sea
I cannot wait to get home
Into your arms.

**Georgina Thomas (10)**
Heavers Farm Primary School

## Buried

I was unsolved like a mystery
Although it was written in history
What do you think I am, a
*Fool?*
If I was rich I would've gone to school
I was in a war
My bones felt so sore
Even though we had a cannonball
I felt so small.

**Reiss Goodridge**
**Heavers Farm Primary School**


## The Tomcat

Tomcat's eyes are like sizzling stars
Tomcat's teeth are like razor blades
Tomcat's claws are like sharpened pencils
Tomcat's whiskers are like silky cream
Tomcat's growl is like a lion's roar
Tomcat's run is like a cheetah's
Tomcat's fur is like a soft blanket.

**David Layne (9)**
**Heavers Farm Primary School**


## What It Feels Like To Be At Sea

Floating away in the deep blue sea!
Waves crashing against the ship
Betrayed, scared and alone
As I sail to a completely different island
And all the way home.

**Karis Weller (11)**
**Heavers Farm Primary School**

## The Blitz

I was frightened,
I was scared,
I felt like hiding under the stairs.

I was shaking in my boots,
As the bombs rained down,
I ran to my shelter,
Deep under ground.

My dad put the air raid sirens on,
Because we were going to get bombed,
People ran to their shelter,
Deep under ground.

**Myles Shaw (10)**
**Heavers Farm Primary School**


## The Snow

Excitement rising,
See the sky.
Big snow coming,
Spraying over the building.

Frozen floors,
Never stopping.
Big snow coming,
Spraying over buildings.

People slipping,
Snowman making,
Slushy over the building.

Snow clouds coming,
Icy building.
Spraying over the buildings,
See through icicles,
Snow on our roof!

**Neruja Sakthikumaran (7)**
**Holbeach Primary School**

## Snow Has Come

Snowflakes falling
On buildings and houses
People shout, 'Hooray
It's snowing, it's snowing.'

Icicles dropping
Car crashes happening
People shout, 'Hooray
It's snowing, it's snowing.'

Brothers dancing
Making angels
People shout, 'Hooray
It's snowing, it's snowing.'

Sky is white
No more clouds
People shout, 'Hooray
It's snowing, it's snowing.'

**Hassan Aktunch (8)**
Holbeach Primary School


## Blowing

Slammed the door
Excitement coming
Winds are blowing
Sweeping over the park
Put on gloves
Wrap round scarves
Winds are blowing
Sweeping over the park
Winds rising
Pull hoods up
Run out to play
Winds are blowing
Sweeping over the park.

**Marcus Angel (7)**
Holbeach Primary School

## Snow Coming

Put on hats
Put on coats
Run outside
Big snow coming

Kids playing
Snowman making
Snowball throwing
Big snow coming

Icicle puddles
Snowman making
Cars slipping
Kids throwing snowballs
Big snow coming.

**Karling Morriss (7)**
Holbeach Primary School

## Spin In The Sky

People screaming, treetops blowing
Tornadoes flying over trees
Neighbours gather
People running, treetops blowing
Tornadoes flying over trees
Neighbours gather.

**Alana Falconer-Lawson (7)**
Holbeach Primary School

## Snow Is Here

Excitement rising
See the sky
Snow clouds coming
Floating over the buildings.

Snow falling
Snuggle up warm
Snow clouds coming
Floating over the buildings.

Having fun
Never stopping
Snow clouds coming
Floating over the buildings.

Snowball throwing
Snowman making
Fingers numbing
Toes tingling
Snow blizzard is here
Covering the buildings.

**Rachea Allen (8)**
**Holbeach Primary School**


## Walking Down The High Street

I am walking down the high street
There are lots of people with bags of clothes
When I went to the shop they were all shut
I went to another high street
There are lots of people
But not a lot of clothes.

**Soner Mustafa**
**Holbeach Primary School**

## Who Took The Button?

Who took the button?
Who took the button?
Who took the button?

Me no, no
Where could it be?

Nobody move
Injured button
On the floor
It is broken.

Oh! Crumbs
Why are we
Standing here?

Get the phone
Call the ambulance.

**Jessie Palmer (8)**
**Holbeach Primary School**


## Yummy Pizza

Yummy, yummy pizza
So likeable I can't forget
Crusty, cheesy don't forget
I can't believe it
Hmmm let me see
I think it's spicy or is it cheesy?
It must be so yummy
Which to choose
*Hrrrrrrr, hmmmmm*
*Eureka!*

**Phernell Davis-Senior (8)**
**Holbeach Primary School**

## Ambushed

Animals are fleeing
Birds are gleaming
While fish sense no fear
Dolphins are jumping
While whales are thumping
As the little deer finds its way
Rhinos are bashing
But elephants are crashing.
One falls behind but one dined
As his feast is on the way.

**Lewis Stewart (11)**
**Holbeach Primary School**


## Reading Books

I like reading
it's great fun.
When you read you learn
books bring enjoyment
to you and me.
Sometimes they make you sad
and sometimes they make you happy
but they are always interesting.

**Kirsty Hopkins (8)**
**Holbeach Primary School**

## That's Impossible

'I saw a chocolate house
with an icing roof.'

'No you never you big fibber!'

'I saw a magic foot
with blue and red toes.'

'No you never you big fibber!'

'I saw a colourful duck in the red sea
with her babies.'

'No you never you big fibber,
that's impossible!'

'I saw a donkey sting a monster
with his tail.'

'No you never you big fibber!'

**Shannon Marshall (7)**
**Holbeach Primary School**


## Ridiculous

'I saw a fierce crocodile with a wooden leg.'
'In your dreams.'
'I did
I saw a four-legged octopus going into the sea.'
'In your dreams.'
'I did
I saw a grey cockroach with millions of hairs.'
'In your dreams.'
'I did
I saw a flying cat with a hamster going round and round.'

**Nadine Thompson Best (7)**
**Holbeach Primary School**

## That Can Never Be True

'I saw a skinny pig
singing to a mic.'

'No you never! You silly liar!'

'I did.
I saw a fat lion shaving his hair.'

'No you never! You silly liar!'

'I did.
I saw a magic carpet
trying to catch a bunch of ants.'

'No you never! You silly liar!'

'I did.
I saw a tiger looking for a boy
all around the jungle yard.'

'No you never! You silly liar!'

'I did.
I saw a man throwing a leopard in the bin.'

'No you never! You silly liar!'

**Stepha-Kay McCarthy (7)**
Holbeach Primary School


## The Funniest Jokes In The World

'I saw a scary dragon with fire coming from his ears.'
'No you never you big joker!'
'I saw a green crocodile with extra sharp teeth.'
'No you never you big joker!'
'I saw a chocolate house with skinny dolls inside.'
'No you never you big joker!'
'I saw a werewolf eating with his claws.'
'No you never you big joker!'
'I saw a big fish swimming with its fin.'
'No you never you big joker!'

**Brandon Carby-Wilson (7)**
Holbeach Primary School

## That Can't Be True

'I saw a chocolate house with mustard and cream.'
'No you never! You big liar?'
'I did
I saw a wrinkly granny with sixteen toes.'
'No you never! You big liar!'
'I did
I saw a pink gorilla that was playing football.'
'No you never! You big liar!'
'I did
I saw a red dragon with painted toenails.'
'No you never! You big liar!'
'I did
I saw Rapunzel with spotted pyjamas.'
'No you never! You big liar!'
'I did.'

**Molly Wole-Ajibode**
**Holbeach Primary School**


## Impossible Poems

'I saw a magic dragon
That went to human school.'
'No you never, fibber!'
'I saw a blue and red Pokémon
With lots and lots of babies.'
'No you never, fibber!'
'I saw a blue knight
With a chocolate star.'
'No you never, fibber!'
'I saw a stupid man
With quite a lot of beans.'
'No you never, fibber!'
I saw a clever doctor
That does lots and lots of science.'
'No you never, fibber!'

**Daniel Jeremy (8)**
**Holbeach Primary School**

## Hamsters

Hamsters, hamsters
those little lazy bones.
Hamsters, hamsters
they like playing with balls.
Hamsters, hamsters
they like rolling in their cage.
Hamsters, hamsters
they like tasting different food.
Hamsters, hamsters
they like nibbling stuff.
Hamsters, hamsters
they bite strangers.
Hamsters, hamsters
they've got a nice warm house.
Hamsters, hamsters
they are really loving.
Hamsters, hamsters.

**Abirami Thangarajah (8)**
**Holbeach Primary School**


## When I Go To Football

When I go to football
I run and slip
I kick the ball
Yes I scored a goal
People pushing and hugging
It's half-time
I come back out
All of them are pushing
I fall down
Oh no we lost.

**Bilal Butt (9)**
**Holbeach Primary School**

## Football

Goals, ball falls
Free kick
People
Pitch, rich
Crowd, proud, loud
Referee
Blows his whistle
Linesman
Penalty
When they win
The coach runs onto the pitch
And celebrates.

**Mpumi Nxara (8)**
Holbeach Primary School

## Flowers Are Pretty

Flowers are pretty
Flowers are nice
It is like a forest with the hiding mice.
Nibbling, giggling all around
All making a squeaky sound.
The sun is out now,
The mice are jumping up and down
The flowers are dying
They need some water.
I wish flowers had a family
To look after each other.

**Lauron Macauley (8)**
Holbeach Primary School

## Art Shame

Art is fun, often messy
Art is colourful
Art is ordinary
Art is fun
Art is done
Art is the best
Art's from the west
Art is lovely
Art is adorable
So don't be ashamed
When yours is a mess
Just catch the paint
And call
For it's a test
If the police can't catch it
Then yourself
If you paint then
Watch out for the police.

**Nikita Miller (9)**
**Holbeach Primary School**


## Playground Park

The park is noisy, the park is quiet
Parks have dogs barking
The park has squirrels and trees
But it is quiet
In the park people fall off the climbing frame
They climb to the top of the slide
The park is fun.

**Abbey-Gay Brown**
**Holbeach Primary School**

# My Family

There once was a boy called Salar
Who went to Panama
He met a cat and gave him a straw hat
But then ran over him with a car.

There once was a boy who was a brother
He was a brother like no other
He went to a tree
Turned it like a key
And decided to go under cover.

There once was a mum full of great fun
Who had a wonderful son
To the circus she went
And got kind of bent
When she took the elephant's bun.

There once was a cheerful dad
Who went through a funny fad
He wore purple clothes
And a ring through his nose
Until his wife said,
'No! You look too mad!'

**Salar Rezaian (9)**
Holbeach Primary School


# That Can't Be True!

'I saw a short dragon with flames that looked like the sun.'
'No you never.'
'I did
I saw a giant mouse that ate the moon.'
'No you never.'
'I did.'

**Hassan Butt (8)**
Holbeach Primary School

## Sleepovers

Sleepovers, sleepovers
All of them are fun.
We all go outside and play under the sun.

Sleepovers, sleepovers
We all tell a joke.
In the bath where we soak.

Sleepovers, sleepovers
We all like to be amused
But then tiredness makes us confused.

Sleepovers, sleepovers
We all feel lazy
So tired our parents think we're crazy.

**Gabriella Bent (9)**
**Holbeach Primary School**


## I Love School

School is where I go each day
When I'm there I learn and play
Playtimes can be good fun
But not when there's rain instead of sun
Art is my favourite thing to do
Writing stories I like too
Each day in assembly we all meet
Some days it's a bore, sometimes it's a treat
In maths we work with numbers galore
I do like school I do I'm sure!

**Sophia Elliott (8)**
**Holbeach Primary School**

## Flowers

Flowers are beautiful
Flowers are fun
They look lovely in the morning sun
Flowers grow in all colours
Who could ever say no
To having flowers out on show.

Flowers are just the best
Some flowers grow with hair
And some flowers grow in a pair.

When I see flowers
I want to kiss them
But if you pick them
They will die
So please don't do it
Please try.

**Natalie Palmer (8)**
**Holbeach Primary School**

## Chocolate Thought

Imagine a Milky Way
as big as a king-sized bed,
appearing in your room
cracking the lovely chocolate
scraping the gooey inside
eating it with your hands.

**Rhianna Minott**
**Holbeach Primary School**

## Cheesy Weesy

'I saw a purple leopard
With a green hat.'
'No you never! That's impossible!'
'I did.
I saw a walking dolls' house
With tree trunks for legs.'
'No you never! That's impossible!'
'I did.
I saw a chocolate house
With mustard and cream.'
'No you never! That's impossible!'
'I did!
I saw a green dinosaur
With one toe.'
'No you never! That's impossible!'

**Taylor Johnson (7)**
Holbeach Primary School


## Mummies

Mummies are a nuisance
Mummies are so loud
Mummies are annoying
Mummies make a crowd
Mummies are a pain
Mummies are so slow
Mummies are kind
If you ever need a hug
They never say no!

**Katie Talbot (8)**
Holbeach Primary School

## Never

'I saw a hat and a half.'
'An eagle doing DJ mix.'
'You never.'
'I did
I saw a black bean fish
Doing a double back flip.'
'You never.'
'I saw a black eagle
Reading an encyclopaedia.'
'You never.'
'I did
I saw a lion playing Buckaroo.'
'You did?'

**Nelson Hylton (7)**
**Holbeach Primary School**


## Football

Playing football every Sunday
Scoring goals now and then
The other team cheats
So they end up winning.

I slide tackle and get dirty
People shouting and noisy
I love scoring goals and winning
The other team argues
With the winning team.

**Lee Cornford (8)**
**Holbeach Primary School**

## That Can't Be True!

'I saw a raisin house
With a pointed nose.'
'No you never! You liar!'
'I did!
I saw a chocolate bar
With some toenails.'
'No you never! You liar!'
'Also I saw a skinny cat
That had crumbled eyes.'
'No you never!'
'I did!
I saw a guitar
With a glue stick tongue.'
'No you never!'
'I did!
I saw a greedy fox
That had a coconut head!'
'No you never!'
'I did!
I saw a collar and it even spoke!'
'You did?'

**Sarah Adebayo (7)**
**Holbeach Primary School**


## Liar

I saw a red dragon with painted toenails
I saw a red monster and he ate the moon
I saw a magic crystal with shining stars
I saw a blue griffin with a fluffy head
I saw a flying window with a lion on the sill
I saw a lion and it was cutting its hair.

**Joshua Reid (8)**
**Holbeach Primary School**

# Impossible!

'I saw a red snail
With a fluffy shell.'
'That's impossible!'
'I saw a talking apple
With 20 legs.'
'That's impossible!'
'I saw a green rose
With a red spotty stem.'
'That's impossible!'
'I saw an ugly princess
Saying I'm so pretty.'
'That's impossible!'

**Duyen Tran (7)**
**Holbeach Primary School**


# It's Ridiculous

'I saw a massive tiger
Blowing in the wind.'
'No you never! You liar!'
'I did!
I saw a small plug
With a very tinsy head.'
'No you never! You liar!'
'I did!
I saw a chocolate plane
In the chocolate sky.'
'No you never! You liar!'
'I did!'

**Dana Baines (8)**
**Holbeach Primary School**

## Senses

I see the gazebo
Wooden
Like a shed.

I hear a train,
Ch, ch, ch
Like a long snake.

I feel the sun
Hot,
Like a light.

I smell the air,
Cold
Like Evian water.

**Gio Paris (6)**
**Holbeach Primary School**


## Impossible!

'I saw a golden crocodile
With fire from its mouth.'
'That's impossible!'
'I saw a little man
And his name was Rumpelstiltskin.'
'That's impossible!'
'I saw a colourful ark
With 150 animals.'
'That's impossible.'

**Boriana Ivanova (8)**
**Holbeach Primary School**

## All Alone

Some animals fleeing
Some not seeing
It was my chance to run
As I heard the sound of a gun

I went to hide
And then I cried
Will they come home soon?
For the strike of the early moon
I loved my mum and dad

He was a great lad
I went to my place
And remembered my parents' faces
They came back
With a bigger pack.

**Ashley Salmon (10)**
**Holbeach Primary School**


## Our Playground

I see the drain
square
like the sweetshop floor.

I hear some people
noisy and loud
like Lewisham Centre.

I feel the wind
blowing
like a hair dryer.

I smell flowers
lemon
like spray polish.

**Jake Miller (6)**
**Holbeach Primary School**

## Our Senses

I see a patball wall
colourful
like a rainbow.

I hear a train
chuckling
like little people.

I feel a bird's house
hard and rough
like bricks in the classroom.

I smell the fresh air
salty
like the sea.

**Sophie Merrill (7)**
**Holbeach Primary School**


## Need A Friend

I was in the park all alone
Clouds going by
With mist on the ground
Mixed with snow I was
Scared I had no friends
I hate being alone
I need someone with me
I can hear funny noises
Around me, it was dangerous
I could hear cars skidding everywhere,
I was scared, all alone.

**Laura Williams (10)**
**Holbeach Primary School**

## All About Senses

I smell the bin
smelly
like somebody passed wind.

I hear the train
bumpy and loud
like a shaker.

I see the school
warm inside
like a haunted house.

I feel the sun
hot and warm
like a hot bath.

**Krystal Bailey (7)**
**Holbeach Primary School**


## Walk In The Park

I see a bin
green
like a pencil.

I feel the ground
bumpy
like rocks.

I hear a plane
smooth
like a bird.

I smell air
cool
like smoke.

**Kavina Narayah (7)**
**Holbeach Primary School**

## Dizzy

I see the gazebo
yellow and shady
like a shadow.

I hear a car,
loud and roaring
like a train going through a tunnel.

I smell the bin,
stale, old food
like dying flowers.

I feel the sun,
hot
like a hot bath.

**Reece-Danielle Abbott (7)**
Holbeach Primary School

## Senses

I see blossom
pink and small
like flowers.

I hear children
noisy and everywhere
like instruments playing.

I smell the air
natural and cold
like smoke.

I feel the wall
bumpy and knotted
like wood.

**Jamie-Lee Ingram (7)**
Holbeach Primary School

## Senses

I see a football pitch
concrete, fake
like a pavement.

I hear a car
loud, moving
like a train but not like an earthquake.

I smell the air
smooth,
like a cold nose.

I feel a tree
hard, tall
like my dad.

**Cairo Duhaney-Burton (7)**
Holbeach Primary School

## The Trip

I see a tree,
bent and old,
spiky.

I hear a train,
dirty and smelly,
rusty.

I smell the air,
cold and windy,
frosty.

I feel the floor,
hard, crusty.

**Zhané McKenzie (6)**
Holbeach Primary School

## Senses

I see a gazebo
circular
like a sunshade of a wooden house.

I hear a train
smooth
like a foot rubbing on a playground floor.

I smell Tic-Tacs
minty
like chewing gum toothpaste.

I feel a stone floor
bumpy
like slippery snowshoes.

**Naomi Howell (6)**
**Holbeach Primary School**


## Explain Words

I see trees
tall and spiky
like people.

I hear an aeroplane
taking the wind
like an old bird.

I feel the ground
all bubbles
like in a bath.

I smell flowers
fresh
like cream.

**Théo Merlin (6)**
**Holbeach Primary School**

## Our Senses

I see the wood gate
hard, hard, hard
like ash.

I hear a train
thundering
like a big van.

I feel moss
cold
like furry sand.

I smell air
damp
like a clearing.

**Sebastian Elliott (6)**
**Holbeach Primary School**


## Aeroplanes

Aeroplanes racing
Aeroplanes tracing
Aeroplanes following
Aeroplanes carrying
Aeroplanes tracking
Aeroplanes landing
Aeroplanes taking
Aeroplanes flying
Aeroplanes trying
Aeroplanes working
Aeroplanes changing
Aeroplanes raging
Last of all . . .
Aeroplanes spacing.

**Liam Moroney (9)**
**Holbeach Primary School**

## My Pet Fish

My pet fish
are orange and brown
My pet fish
are happy and swim around
My pet fish
live in a tank
My pet fish
are spotty
My pet fish
have fins and tails
My pet fish
like to eat and eat
My pet fish
come to me
I had lots of fish but now
they're mostly dead,
but I still love my fish.

**Eliz Hassan (9)**
**Holbeach Primary School**


## London

This is my life . . .

My mum is loving,
My dad is kind and generous
My sisters are lovely
My brothers are sweet
My friends are very good
My teachers are the best
I am helpful
My grandpa is special
My grandma is beautiful
My auntie is happy
My uncle is smart
That's the end of my life for now.

**Jade Angela Kidd (8)**
**Holbeach Primary School**

## Exams

I have an anxious feeling trapped inside,
Exams always send a shiver down my spine.
Haunting my thoughts which pass through my brain.
Exams always give some kind of pain.

Exams leave a tingling feeling in my mind,
There always is a fear sticking by my side.
Can't you make this feeling just go away?
I want to be normal and be able to play.

My mind is frozen. I cannot think!
I want it to go as quick as a blink.
It is always exams, exams, exams.
Is the world made of anything more than exams?

**Lorella Couch (10)**
Holbeach Primary School

## Camp Choir

All around the camp fire
People singing like a choir
Singing loud
Singing proud
Singing high
Singing low
Making all the animals go.

**Ceylan Mustafa (10)**
Holbeach Primary School

## My Cousin

My cousin is fast but she
always comes last

She hates me but she
always has to date me

She's strong and she
sings a song

She's bad and she
always gets mad

She's tall and good
at basketball

She likes boys and
their toys

She's late for food
on her plate.

**Ashley Lewis (8)**
**Holbeach Primary School**


## Sam

There once was a boy called Sam
Who had a diet of bread and ham
It ached in his belly
Then the air turned all smelly
And boy how the townspeople ran.

**David Welch (8)**
**Holbeach Primary School**

## My Family

My name is Makeda and I can
be a tease.
I have four sisters who love
the pictures.
My sister Sienna always asks
for her dinner.
My sister Tia is always
a cheater.
My sister Akira is always
staring.
My sister Emeka thinks
she's always the leader.
My little cat Smudge always
holds a grudge.
My mum is fun and Dad is fab,
I'm glad I wrote on this piece
of sheet, 'cause my family is
so sweet.

**Makeda Roberts (8)**
**Holbeach Primary School**


## Butterfly Wing

Butterfly, butterfly
Colourful and bright,
Makes me feel so lucky and happy.
Stripy and spotty, lined with colours,
Flaps their wing and looks just right
To reach the heights.
Fly, fly, flat butterfly
Fly like an angel in the sky.

**Vanessa Adetunji (8)**
**Holbeach Primary School**

## Arsenal

Arsenal never had lost in the season,
Arsenal, Arsenal,
Arsenal have got the best player called Henry.
Arsenal, Arsenal.
Arsenal chose Frances to be their captain.
Arsenal, Arsenal
Sol Campbell is a good defender.
Arsenal, Arsenal.
Sometimes Robert Pierre scores for France.
Arsenal, Arsenal
Arsenal is a good team in the League.
Arsenal, Arsenal
Arsenal, so skilled because of the player Thierry Henry.

**Kaner Scott (8)**
**Holbeach Primary School**


## The High Street

A road like a grey river,
Stormy clouds in the sky.
People running into shops to get
Out of the rain.
Watery shoes walking on the
Wet pavements.
Cars are driving over wet roads.
People's hoods get blown down
By the wind.

**Michael Crawley (8)**
**Holbeach Primary School**

## The High Street

Roads looking like a grey river,
Lots of vehicles floating along.
People hiding from the rain,
People buying umbrellas, hoods up,
Trees rustling, moving with the wind.
People walking but splashing at the same time.
People smoking.
Engines to be smelt.
Bins smell.
Barking dogs,
People with bags and bags of shopping.
Lovely smells of food.
Rubbish on the floor.

**Samantha Sharpe (8)**
Holbeach Primary School


## Football Crazy

A football as round as a human head
A player as tall as a goal
The crowd as excited as a boy opening his presents
The ref, as happy as a popstar
The players as rich as a millionaire
The football pitch, as dirty as a pig rolling in mud
The teams are as skilled as a gymnastic person
The trainers as mashed up as a dead person
The teams scoring a goal whilst the crowd do a Mexican wave
The ref giving out yellow and red cards.

**Avision Ho (9)**
Holbeach Primary School

## Horses

Horses, horses
Trip, trap, trot
Make me happy from the lot.
They get some hay in the middle of May
Working lots.
They get so hot
I like their manes
But they don't eat their grain
Their noses are soft and they
Never get lost.

**Weronica Basia Bozzao (8)**
Holbeach Primary School

## A Poem About Football

I love playing football because
it's really fun,
I love playing football because
it gets me fit.
My favourite team is *Arsenal!*
*'Go on my son!'*
And my brother thinks I'm mad
because I say that!
All the players in the team are so talented
but not as good as *me!*

**Tchaan Wilson-Townsend (9)**
Holbeach Primary School

## Terrified

The scaly, big black thing emerged from the dark corner
Its long hairy legs moving suddenly
The way it moved jagged her mind and she realised . . .
That it was a spider
Her mind started to spin
Bits of information flew out of her head.
All she could do, think or see was a great immeasurable spider . . .
The spider moved a little, information flew back to her head
She knew what she had to do,
But she couldn't
She could not just dash for the door
She was too frightened
And she knew that when she came back
The spider would be there
Before she could stop herself she flew to the door
Just when she thought it was over
She felt something slimy under her shoe?
She had stepped on the spider!

**Jade Beason (11)**
**Holbeach Primary School**

## Alone

Alone in the foggy wood
No one around
And not even a sound
Then something comes
He looks for his feast
It looks nasty, like a beast.

**Georgia Farley (11)**
**Holbeach Primary School**

## Too Much Pain

He treated me like dirt
And it really, really hurt
He caused me so much pain
And the memories are in my brain

He took my dinner money
And he thought it was funny
The suffering he caused
It never ever paused

You thought you were bad
But you just made me sad
You thought I was not like you
But I have feelings too!

**Paisley Thomas (11)**
**Holbeach Primary School**


## About Thierry Henry

He plays for Arsenal
Thierry Henry is an excellent player on the pitch
When he plays on Astroturf
He is the best player in the world.

He has lots of skills,
His team wears red and white
When they play at home
And wear gold and blue when he plays away.

**Theo Batchelor (9)**
**Holbeach Primary School**

## Nightmare

I ran away
Worried as Hell.
I *can* hear something
Something calling my name
*Marlene*.

It is ever so scary.
The world has gone
Black and cold.
But in the middle of the day
How is that possible?

I can see something
I can feel something
I can hear something
What is it?
Who is it?

Who are you?
What are you?
I shout with all my might
It's ever so frightening

Wait a minute
I, I, I . . .
I am at home.
I am in my bed.
It was all a nightmare
Or was it?

**Kaileigh Green (10)**
**Holbeach Primary School**

## Tidying Up

If it drops pick it up
If it spills wipe it up
If it makes a mess sweep it up
If it's too big put it aside
If it is small keep it
If it is dirty clean it

It is good to see those rooms looking tidier
This is to let you know that tidying your room is a good thing
It makes your room smell good and for once, it is clean . . .

**Rosie Mgbeike (9)**
Holbeach Primary School

## Swimming

The day I learnt to swim
Was a struggle
But I didn't give up
I was worried that
I would drown

I have started to make great progress
And I have been swimming my heart out
I'm happy I've learnt now
So I won't be left out.

**Lithasa Puvanenthirarasa (11)**
Holbeach Primary School

## The Ghost

It entered on a foggy night
The room went cold I turned on the light
There it stood a ghost at the door
It said it wanted a talk and nothing more
I sat there scared and petrified
But it only glared and tried to hide
It stopped hiding and floated over to my bed
I was glad I wasn't dead

Its eyes glowed red its teeth were black
Then it held up a giant sack
Full of hands and heads it was
The ghost grabbed at me with its claws
I screamed for help all I did was yelp and yelp
Mum and Dad came rushing in
Dad ran so fast he bumped into the bin
The ghost was gone and Mum and Dad
Said it was a dream so I was glad.

**Echo Carnell (10)**
**Holbeach Primary School**


## Swimming

The day I learnt to swim a thrill
My arms were splashing all about
I tried and tried
But nothing happened
My legs started to hurt
I wanted to give up
I tried one more time
I began to make progress
My heart started beating faster
With excitement.
Now I swim very well
I don't think of drowning.

**Yashar Aktunch (11)**
**Holbeach Primary School**

## Snake

Walking in the jungle
Lost in the jungle
I saw a snake slithering past
So I followed it to see, to see
Of where to find water
Making me hopeful that I find my home.
I followed it around
All animals would move out the way.
So not to disturb it
It seemed that the snake was the king
Everyone looked at him with respect.
I wanted to drink the cold water
But he took his time.
I could feel the fresh water reaching my lips
But still I had to wait
Making me every more thirsty!

**Tobi Olusola (10)**
Holbeach Primary School


## Free

Can't you see
There's a wish to be free

They don't want to be caged up
Or genetically made up

Set them free
Free like a bee

So they can run
In the midday sun

Set them free
Set them free.

**Ellie Veale (11)**
Holbeach Primary School

## Exam Day, Doom Day!

It's here again. Already!
The big black and white thing
With lots of writing
And blank boxes

Why today? I haven't studied
I haven't revised
I haven't done my homework
Why today? Why not tomorrow
Next week, or even next year?

Everyone is getting ready
Fishing in their pencil cases
For pens and good luck teddies
Oh help! What am I going to do?

They're giving out the question papers
People doing the last minute toilet capers
Lost glasses are waiting to be found
Worried bullies doing ten-mile paces . . .

There are no more exams
I thought, I sang
My results were OK, in fact they were brilliant
But then there was a big bang

I heard there was to be another . . . *exam!*

**Hope Mgbeike (11)**
**Holbeach Primary School**

## Climbing

Feeling excited
I climbed the wall
I thought that I was about to fall
I climbed and climbed
I slipped and tripped
But I still carried on
Even though I flopped
I got to the top
I grabbed the rope feeling relieved
And I abseiled down.

**Kieran Daly (11)**
Holbeach Primary School

## Archery

Stretching the bow and
Determined to let it go
It wasn't very scary
But very exciting
Standing to the side and
Pulling it right back
To my cheek
It hurt a bit
But for the whole week.

**Joshua Andrews-Smith (11)**
Holbeach Primary School

## Scared

The shiver down your spine
When you're walking down the road
All alone, in the cold
The feeling that you're being watched
Even though the road is empty,
Just so quiet, that's what's scary.
A gigantic, silent, empty place,
Your footsteps echoing off the walls.
Checking around you, hunting for the face
That is following you, watching you
There's no one there, you shake your head
But still your heart is thumping,
As you hurry on. Faster than before.
Someone intimidates you.
Who?
No one.
You.
Just you.
All alone. In the dark.
With your fears.

**Caitlin Campbell (10)**
Holbeach Primary School

## Climbing

I was about the climb the wall.
My heart froze!
As I looked up my knees trembling.
The wind gently whistling around my head.
I started to climb slowly
My legs as heavy as lead.
I was getting higher and higher
The top getting nearer and nearer.
Suddenly the sun blazing on my skin
And wow! I had made it.

**Lewis Lang (10)**
Holbeach Primary School

## Remember

Remember the person who cared
Remember the person you scared
Remember the person who cried
Remember the time that you lied

Remember the pain and the fear
Remember the watery tears
Remember the time when you pushed and kicked
Remember the time when you slapped and hit

I still remember how you shouted and you lied
I still remember how you hurt me inside
I still remember getting hurt 'cause I was tall
I still remember wishing that I was small

You hurt me so bad
And when you did you were glad
If you were here now I would show you my pain
'Cause although it was ages ago nothing has changed.

**Lakisha Henderson (10)**
**Holbeach Primary School**

## Kick Ups

Feeling fantastic
Running out to play
The sun is shining
On a lovely day.

Feeling ashamed of people in front of me
Only two
Then three
Slowly becoming twenty-three.

Feeling excited
Running out to play
The rain is pouring
On a bad, bad day
Maybe I'll play on another day.

**Hareesh Balendra (10)**
**Holbeach Primary School**

## Ice Skating

Pain ran through me,
I just wanted to flee.

Holding onto the railing,
Because I just kept failing.

I was really cold,
But I knew I had to be bold.

I knew I had the power,
But my mouth tasted sour.

I started to skate,
I felt great!

It felt so easy
And I wasn't freezing.

**Dean Ferraro (11)**
**Holbeach Primary School**


## Our Senses

I see children playing
fast, loud, noisy
like a motorbike.

I feel wind blowing my mouth
dry, dry, dry
like I wanted juice.

I hear trains
fast, fast, fast
like a house and thunder.

I smell Tic-Tacs
minty Tic-Tacs
like an inhaler.

**Seun Olatunde (7)**
**Holbeach Primary School**

## There's A Fire In The School

There's a fire in the school
The drill is ringing loudly
The children are all screaming
Teachers feel drowsy

There's a fire in the school
It's crackling like mad
Some people are glad
That the fire's dying down

There's a fire in the school
The firefighters are not here
The school is not clear
To see if it is still here

There's a fire in the school
They are here at last
The water is going to blast
And the school has stopped
Its mighty *flames*.

**Lauren Lazic-Duffy (10)**
**Holbeach Primary School**


## Frightened

F ire, fire
R ushing to my nest
I ncredibly fast
G rowling and heat against my chest
H iding I am doing
T ime and time again my baby is chewing,
E nding time I do not know
N ow I can't see because of the fire
E very time I look round the smoke gets higher
D on't like it, can't take it.

**Nicole Lawson (10)**
**Holbeach Primary School**

## Skiing

Standing on pieces of wood,
Scared but excited,
Cold but hot inside,
Sliding down
Is so scary,
I need strength
And energy,
My fingers are numb,
My feet are the same,
I might fall off,
Or lose control,
It might be all those things.
But once you know,
It's fine and great fun.

**Anaïs Merlin (10)**
Holbeach Primary School

## Swimming

I dipped in the freezing water
Nervous and excited
I flapped and flapped
Going nowhere
I dived and tried
But got nowhere
My dad threw me in
I sank until I got saved
I tried the water slide
I went under water
I ended up swimming.

**Gokan Emirali (11)**
Holbeach Primary School

## Spider

It's in the corner of my room
It sends shivers down my spine
With cobwebs and flies
All stuck in its line

It's the eight-legged freak
From far away
It's as black as ebony
It sends my mind astray

It's the nightmare from Hell
It makes me petrified
Go away, go away!
You make me feel terrified

I'd rather be underground
Like a miner
I'm afraid of a big, fat, hairy *spider!*

**Sharna McKenzie (11)**
Holbeach Primary School


## A Walk Outside

I see the gate
metal and black
like an open escape.

I hear a train
loud and rushing
like the wind.

I feel the bricks
hard and rough
like cement.

I smell the bin
disgusting, slimy
like a boy.

**Amaju Ayonronmi (6)**
Holbeach Primary School

## Sneaky Adder

I lay, in the mild, yet warm, sunshine, in my hammock
With a sombre expression, very sombre, upon my face
I mourn, so mournfully, one so mortally wounded
By the venomous, intangible adder!

Glowering at his hidey-hole, still unaware of danger,
I think how one's life will never be spared,
By the deadly bite, oh, the venomous bite,
Of the venomous, intangible adder!

I am getting the least of sleep, now aware that the adder,
The poisonous demon of spring, with glowering, leering eyes,
Is about to slither out of that hideaway place,
Ready to pounce on me any second,
I am easy prey, easy, easy prey.

With the traumatising venom in his fangs,
He slithers up to me, about to paralyse me!
I scream, a blood-curdling, heart shattering scream,
As his fangs are inserted through my skin, into my bloodstream!

And I grab the snake, delirious with poison,
But drop the now tangible adder,
As a virus is gnawing away at my health and strength.

And as I lay dying, crying, trying,
Just unable to make an attempt to stay alive,
I ask, will I see the light of another day again?

**Emma-Louise Bullions (10)**
Holbeach Primary School

## Camp

Camps are fun
When eating bun,
Sleeping in tents,
Smelling burning scents
But most of all camps are great
And most of the time you make a mate.

**Jamila Francis (11)**
Holbeach Primary School

## We Went To The Park

I see an aeroplane
with gliding wings
like a golden bird.

I hear a train
noisy, fast
like a white car.

I feel the wind
crunchy cold
like snow.

I smell flowers
hot
like vegetables on the table.

**Savannah Harrison (6)**
**Holbeach Primary School**


## In The Playground

I see the drain
square
like a monster's mouth.

I hear people
talking loud
like an elephant.

I feel the wind
cold
like a monster's cough.

I smell orange skin
sweet
like a fizzy flower.

**Chelsea Scott (6)**
**Holbeach Primary School**

## Snow Blizzard

Excitement rising
See the sky
Huge clouds coming
Laying over the buildings.

Snowflakes dropping
Snowflakes gathering
Huge clouds coming
Laying over the buildings.

Children gathering
Building snowmen
Fluffy clouds coming
Laying over the buildings.

Snow on the city
Clouds blowing
Snowflakes whizzing
Children shouting
Huge snow blowing
Blizzard! on the buildings.

**Sasha Agyeman-Dwommah (8)**
Holbeach Primary School


## Fear

Fear is everywhere
Even while we're lying here
Like a gunshot
Banging like a door knock.
Is that all that is left?
Hurt and death
Like a gunshot
Banging like a door knock.

**Jensen Brown (10)**
Holbeach Primary School

## Alone In The Woods

Alone in the woods
Abandoned forlorn
Crying for help but no use
Eyes gleaming round
What could it be, danger?
Innocent eyes starring back at me
Waiting for the right moment
To pounce straight there
Wishing it would go away
But all excitement
For a newborn deer.

**Melissa Virassamy (10)**
**Holbeach Primary School**


## Bat Ups

I'm really excited
Bat ups for the first day.
Let's come and play
On a day like this.

Very bad for the first day
Only managing to do two,
Then four I want to do more.

Next day ten,
Then twenty.

**Wajid Hassan (11)**
**Holbeach Primary School**

## Thunderbolt

Thunderbolt coming
Wind blowing
Cars slipping, snow falling
Coming up the mountain.

Screaming children
Adult sleeping
Snow falling
Coming up the mountain.

Shut the window
Shut the door
Thunderbolt is about to crash the place.
Big breeze is coming
Coming up the mountain.

Thunderbolt coming
Wind swishing
Snow falling
Thunderbolt on the mountain.

**Kieran Lang (7)**
**Holbeach Primary School**


## Dancing Flames

Fires are dangerous, but magical to watch.
The crackling noises, the sparks flying
And the dancing flames.
The colours are beautiful, but too hot to touch.
But when the dancing flames die cold,
Black ashes are the only things that are left behind.

**Kyle Mekarssi (10)**
**Holbeach Primary School**

## Snow Blizzard

Gazing through windows
Everyone cheer hooray
Rooftops white
Snow blizzard blowing.

Coats on quickly
Run outside
Snowball throwing
Snow blizzard blowing.

Icicles dropping
Snowman making
Frozen ice puddles
Big snow blizzard blowing.

Pretty snow angels
Slippery ground
Snowflakes falling
Never stopping
See-through icicles
Windy snow storm.

**Tyler Cox (8)**
**Holbeach Primary School**


## Snow Storm

Snowy clouds coming
Rising over the rooftops
Fierce wind sweeping
Through the trees
People throwing snowballs
At each other
Fierce winds sweeping
Through the trees
Children making snowmen
Carrot for a nose
Big blizzard coming
Through the trees.

**Raeon McKenzie-Abbott (7)**
**Holbeach Primary School**

## Snow Is Fun

Excitement coming,
Something dropping,
What is it?
Snow!
Big drops of snow,
Snow is falling on your head,
People running to the park
Throwing snow all about the place.
Big drops splashing,
Big snow drizzling,
Rushing to the park,
Skating to the park,
Everybody loves snow.

**Ernest Adadevoh (8)**
**Holbeach Primary School**


## The Snow

White clouds are coming to snow on us in the winter.
The snow is coming to us and it is fast.
The clouds are rising up the sky at night to snow down.
The clouds are rising up to the sky in the morning
To snow down on us.
Snow falling, snowmen-making in the snow,
Fingers freezing in the snow, snow falling down,
Snow on the rooftops, the snow is falling over the roofs
And the building,
The snow clouds are opening to snow on us in the morning.
The snow is falling outside in the garden
And we are making snowmen in the garden.

**Mariam Gul (8)**
**Holbeach Primary School**

## I Love Snow

Thunderbolt coming
Snowflakes falling
So exciting
Quickly, quickly, quickly
Put on gloves.

Making snow angels
Throwing snowballs
So exciting
Quickly, quickly, quickly
Put on gloves.

Never stopping
That's good
Come on
Let's go outside
So exciting
Quickly, quickly, quickly
Put on gloves.

**Ebony Okuonghae (8)**
Holbeach Primary School

## Fire Flames

Dark night ground roaring
Flames blazing and dancing
While the trees are gathering
Animals fleeing the wind
Driving through the flames
While the fishes swim in the sea
And the flames spread round the forest.

**Omer Bozdog (10)**
Holbeach Primary School

## Winter Weather

Snow is coming
put on warm clothes
start up the fire.
Snow is coming
put on warm clothes.

Coats on quick
run outside
make a snowman with a hat.
Snow is coming
put on warm clothes

Gazing through windows
everyone shouts!
Rooftops white.
Snow is coming
everyone shouts, 'Hooray!'

**Danielle Lall (8)**
**Holbeach Primary School**


## Our Senses

I see a frozen puddle
hard and cracked
like a see-through window.

I hear a train
banging and crackling
like a tram.

I smell a drain
dirty
like an air vent.

I feel the wind
cold and invisible
like a ghost.

**Adetunji Iwala (7)**
**Holbeach Primary School**

## Senses

I see a climbing frame
round, metal
like a monster.

I hear instruments
loud, banging
like drums.

I smell daffodils
green, straight
like being asleep.

I feel cold air
invisible
like the wind.

**Rodney Abbey (6)**
**Holbeach Primary School**


## Our Playground

I see the climbing frame
big
like a monster.

I hear a aeroplane
vrooming
like a bird.

I feel the floor
hard
like wood.

I touch the basketball net
prickly
like a pin.

**Otaigbeme Aburime (7)**
**Holbeach Primary School**

## Snake

Slithery stopper of life
Not always bad but at their worst
Angry and vicious
Killers and poisoners
Envy and eaters of whatever they find
Spiteful stoppers of life

I met this stopper of life
Slithering around
And spitting poison at the air
And finishing its lunch.
I backed away as it came closer
And spitting in my face
I dropped onto the ground
And then it had its tea!

**Sean Gould (11)**
**Holbeach Primary School**


## The Newborn Deer

Animals are fleeing
None of them are seeing
The fire is winding
The animals are siding
There is all this fear
To save the newborn deer.

**Nicole Sandford (10)**
**Holbeach Primary School**

## One Violent And Silent Night

It was quiet and silent
One night in the dark
I saw something violent
It was like a shark.

But there was no water to be seen
Was it real or was it fake
Or was my imagination a mistake.

**Jazmin Devine   (10)**
**Holbeach Primary School**

## Camping

Wind is blowing
Fire is growing

Foxes are calling
Beetles are crawling

Children are gathering
To hear what a sound

Fire is flaming
It's still not raining.

**Tereece Sewell   (11)**
**Holbeach Primary School**

## Night In The City Streets!

I look down onto the city streets
I see fireflies buzzing around
Surrounding the beetles
Producing a swarm of insects
Then disappearing into the distance.

I feel so happy
Then I see an army
An army of bees and ants in gold jackets
I follow one, a barber
Going to his home from his shop.

Then they collide creating
A war is going on now
The bees and ants are losing,
It's the end of the war.
The beetles are shouting orders to all the slaves, ants and bees
And running away.

**Ehab Ahmed (10)**
**John Ruskin Primary School**


## A Sherbet Lemon For My Five Senses

A sherbet lemon is a sunflower-yellow diamond so precious,
glittering in the light.
A sherbet lemon feels rough to touch, it's a shield,
hard to break through.
A sherbet lemon smells tangy and bitter-lemon sweet.
It's a lemon with sugar poured inside.
A sherbet lemon is a glass of bubbling lemonade.
After I've had it, a sherbet lemon is now a glass of bubbling Coke.
It sounds like me jumping in crunchy, dried up leaves.

**Maxine Agyemang (11)**
**John Ruskin Primary School**

## Help!

Help I'm feeling all these feelings,
I only fell into bed
After my bath like every other night,
They're running through my head.

I look up into the night sky,
Until I realise
That my roof was on hinges,
It's as if I'm hypnotised.

This is what I'm feeling,
I hope it comes out right;
The moon a Milky Button chocolate
In the night sky.

The full everlasting sky,
With twinkling star stones.
Patterns and shapes,
Am I really at home?

**Sophie Walker (11)**
**John Ruskin Primary School**


## My Funny Friends

I have a friend called Millie
who looks quite silly.
She's got a funny nose
like a red rose.
She's got curly hair
like a grizzly bear.
She's got round eyes
like a piece of pie.
She's got a nice chin
like a dirty bin.
Yes, Millie.

**Loretta Otokiti (9)**
**John Ruskin Primary School**

## The Shining Sky

The sun is changing from the bright gold colours
Of the day
To its dark red nightgown ready to start
A new one.
As the moon's alarm clock she gets up
Not in a hurry,
Not in a flurry,
Fetching a curry.
She says, 'Plenty of time to do what I like,
It's not yet time for night.
Aw, it's all right.'
But soon the sun disappears,
I think, *oh cheers, no moon tonight.*
But a pop and a bang,
The stars and the moon appear in a gang,
A big football with loads of crystal tennis balls.
These are the jewels up at a height,
The summer leaves all in a race,
Up in the sky forming a face.
It is not hot, it is not cold then suddenly,
*Zzzz, beep.* Time to wake, time to rise,
'Jack!' I hear my mother cry.

**Jack Lawrance (9)**
John Ruskin Primary School


## All About Mummy

Mummy is so silly.
She's got a long nose
Like a pointy toe.
She's got lovely hair
Like a lovely bear.
She's got wondering eyes
Like a wandering roller coaster.
Guess, who is she?
Her name is Paulina.

**Ruth Boyd (8)**
John Ruskin Primary School

## Stuck In School

Clouds gather outside my window
Scary thunderstorm, wet play today,
Drips drop from the cloudy sky.
What a boring, gloomy, lame day.

Spooky lightning passes by splish-splosh,
Rain is pouring, thunderstorms are getting heavy.
It is dull and getting boring.

Spooky lightning passes by oh!
Me and my mum have a sparky fly.
Thunder coming on the way,
My teacher wants a Milky Way.
People sleeping, people weeping,
Me and my sister are teaching.

**Romoan Oriogun (9)**
John Ruskin Primary School


## Funny Face

She's got a nose
like a hose.
She's got eyes
like a wise fly.
She's got fair hair
like a fair chair.
She's got a skinny chin
like a binny tin.
She's got funky ears
like a wiggly beard.

**Yohannes Kleih (8)**
John Ruskin Primary School

## I Have A Friend Called Millie

I have a friend, Millie
who really looks quite silly,
she's got sticky hair
like a grizzly bear,
she's got big eyes
like two million flies,
she's got an enormous nose
like 3 tremendous toes,
she's got a prickly chin
like sharp pins.

**Alex Julien (8)**
John Ruskin Primary School

## She's Got

I have a friend called Millie
Who really looks quite silly!
She's got a runny nose,
Like a fountain goes.
She's got eyes
Like French fries.
She's got scary hair that
Frightened the bear.
Millie is a sight to see,
But she's as kind as can be.

**Tasnema Raaman (8)**
John Ruskin Primary School

## One Beautiful Night Sky

I'm very dreamy and I don't want to be bothered,
Then all of a sudden the roof is lifted up,
My eyes wander.

Shining bright stars are my diamond earrings glowing in the dark.
The sunset is a calm watercolour painting.
A silhouette is a crowd of shadowy people coming to take me away.
The glistening half moon is a tasty banana,
I can hear the sound of high heels tapping out a tune
I can hear the soft purring of cars in the night.
I feel a fresh sensational warmth in my body.

**Yetunde Adeola (11)**
**John Ruskin Primary School**


## In The Park

Children coming,
Mum talking,
Cars zooming,
Winds arriving,
People screaming,
Fathers racing,
Grandmas burping,
Hurricanes arriving.

**Nkemjika Eka (8)**
**John Ruskin Primary School**

# Our Majestic Dragon
*(Based on 'The Magnificent Bull' from a traditional Dinka tribe in Africa)*

Our dragon is
A rainbow in the sun-drenched sky
Multicoloured like
Smarties decorating the top of a cake,
Multicoloured like
A cloud of balloons,
His back is orange, red and yellow like
Lava trickling down the side of a volcano.
His breath like
Red-hot chillies on top of a pizza.
His teeth jagged like
The edge of a knife cutting cucumbers.
His claws are like
Nails sticking out from floorboards.
His eyes are as golden as
Treasure buried at the bottom of the seven seas.
His tail a
Multicoloured paintbrush gliding across the canvas.
He resembles the world living together in peace and harmony.
We will
Treasure, respect and share him with others,
Our majestic dragon.

**Year 4**
**Lucas Vale Primary School**

## My Magnificent Lion
*(Based on 'The Magnificent Bull' from a traditional Dinka tribe in Africa)*

My magnificent lion is
Light brown like a piece of toast,
Light brown like
The mud and rain mixed together.
His roar is
An earthquake shuddering through the Earth.
He is as fast as
A bullet escaping from the barrel of a gun.
His mane is like
The warmest sheep's wool.
His claws
The sharpest knives, cutting, tearing.
He resembles
His pride living together.
My magnificent lion.

**Steven Viteri (9)**
**Lucas Vale Primary School**

## My Deadly Hornet
*(Based on 'The Magnificent Bull' from a traditional Dinka tribe in Africa)*

His eyes are like . . .
Church stained glass windows.
He is brown like . . .
A steaming hot cup of coffee.
His sting is like . . .
Poison firing from a blowpipe.
His wing like . . .
A silk dressing gown.
He resembles
An aeroplane gliding through the sky.
I will
Train my hornet and share him.
My deadly hornet.

**Sanchez Williams (9)**
**Lucas Vale Primary School**

## My Sparkling Snake
*(Based on 'The Magnificent Bull' from a traditional Dinka tribe in Africa)*

My snake is silver like . . .
The twinkling stars in the bright sky.
Silver like . . .
The shining moon reflecting on the swaying sea.
His mouth as wide as . . .
A huge tunnel waiting to trap a slimy snail.
His tongue as poisonous as . . .
The stem of rhubarb in winter.
His tail is like
A plug wire trembling on the floor.
His back is
Slippery as a litre of water pouring down your back.

He resembles
A superflex ruler.
I will share him with others,
Protect him and train him as
He can get angry and sting others
With his dreadful tongue.
My sparkling snake.

**Ennock Tiemene (8)**
**Lucas Vale Primary School**

## My Brave Eagle
*(Based on 'The Magnificent Bull' from a traditional Dinka tribe in Africa)*

My brave eagle is light brown like . . .
flower stems.
Light brown like . .
someone's skin colour.
Light brown like . . .
Hot toasted currant buns.
His eyes are . . .
Blue like the open ocean.
His wings spread far and wide like . . .
Chinese fans.
His beak is . . .
golden like the sand between your toes.
His cry like . . .
The soothing sound of whales communicating.
He resembles
everyone.

I will set him free to soar and roam
the clear blue sky.
My brave eagle.

**Isabel Rodriguez (9)**
**Lucas Vale Primary School**

## My Precious Cat
*(Based on 'The Magnificent Bull' from a traditional Dinka tribe in Africa)*

My cat is tabby like . . .
Highlights in somebody's hair,
Tabby like
The leaves on a tree in autumn,
She has gold, brown and yellow stripes
like . . .
A tiger's winter coat.
She is
As precious as a newborn baby.
Her purr is like . . .
Birds singing from the treetops.
Her eyes as . . .
Blue as a felt tip pen spreading around the sheet.
She resembles
Peace and tranquillity.
I will
Love, respect and share her.
My precious cat.

**Temitope Ogundipe (8)**
Lucas Vale Primary School

## My Fantastic Dolphin
*(Based on 'The Magnificent Bull' from a traditional Dinka tribe in Africa)*

My dolphin is grey like
the storm cloud in the sky,
Grey like
the hard concrete on the ground.
His skin is like
the smooth ocean glistening in the sunshine.
His beak is hard like
a human bone.
He resembles
helpfulness and kindness.
I will guard, love and cherish him,
my fantastic dolphin.

**Songhay Francis (8)**
Lucas Vale Primary School

# A Nonsense Creature

There's a creature under my bed!
It's big and it's black,
And has a strangely shaped head.

Its colours are amazing,
Its head's as round as a ball,
It's up all day and sleeps at dusk,
But keeps me awake all night!

It chomps and bites,
And has no teeth,
It secretly listens,
But ears, has none!

One night I came to face my fears,
The creature it was,
It did appear,
For a duel it said it was here,
To fight me and then would disappear!

'Of course,' I said, 'I accept your duel.'
They fight would then commence,
Back to back we faced each other,
Drew our swords and shot each other!

**Lucy Sneddon (10)**
Montbelle School

## School Days

Walk to school for ten to nine
Wait in the playground to stand in line,
The teacher takes me into class,
He calls the register very fast.

We have assembly in the hall,
The head teacher speaks to all the school,
After this it's time to play,
The children like this time of day.

We put on our coats and run outside,
We skip, we jump, we run and hide.
It may be cold, it may be hot,
But that won't make us want to stop.

Back in the classroom, work to be done,
It's not always hard, it can be fun.
Different words and numbers too,
We learn a lot from what we do.

We can draw or we may sew,
As long as we just have a go.
It's half-past 3, there's noise and fuss,
The teachers says goodnight to us.

**Alexandra Miller (11)**
**Montbelle School**

## My Cat Brandy

Her soft, silky fur
Is stripy and brown,
Her ears, they prickle,
Her bright eyes glow
Cutting through the darkness.
She stealthily prowls around,
Without a sound,
Her white socked feet,
Pad gently on my legs,
She wobbles up the stairs
And leaps on my bed.
She snuggles in my lap and lies as still as a statue,
Her purrs reverberating through the silence.
Are as loud as thunder,
Her brushed suede under paws gently touch my face,
The sandpaper-like tongue licks my nose with affection,
But then she leaps down onto the floor
And wobbles back down the stairs,
Leaving me alone!

**Amy Watson (10)**
**Montbelle School**

## My Dog

My dog is called Scruffy,
and he is very fluffy.
He runs around the garden,
barking at Mrs Jarden.
When he comes in with his stinky paws,
everyone runs to the shores,
as they know they just might drop dead.
I take him for walks once a day
and extra in May,
because it is his birthday.
His present is normally a bone,
but sometimes he mistakes it for the phone.
We take him to the park in the car,
he stays sitting for long because it is very far.
When we get there we let him free to run around,
sometimes he barks to show us what he has found.
When we get home he is tired,
so he falls into his basket knowing he is admired.

**Tijan N'jai Sealy (10)**
Oakfield Prep School

## Pals

My favourite pals are two cats
Sometimes they look like bats
Black bats.
They eat rats
And sit on mats
That's cats.

Cats are small and furry
Usually they are in a hurry
Wouldn't want them in a curry
That's funny
Black and furry,
My best pals.

**Taylor Johnstone (10)**
Oakfield Prep School

## The Creature

Upon a wall
One moonlit night,
I saw a face, an amazing sight,
Two bright green eyes,
A nose so small,
It could not be human at all,
Two pointed ears coming out of its head
Lying so still as if it were dead,
But then the nose gave a twitch
And it made a sound in a very high pitch,
Then it leapt up, slender and tall,
It was just a cat, that's all.

**Georgina Stenhouse (10)**
Oakfield Prep School

## Spring

Spring has lovely blossoms,
Because of its cheeks and bottom.
That when you look at the grass,
It gives you a lovely wink.
And when you turned round
You thought it actually blinked.
You can smell the fresh blue breeze
It begins to make you sneeze.
And one more thing
You should like,
*Spring!*

**Victoria Dwebeng (11)**
Oakfield Prep School

## Life's Too Short

Starting in a tummy,
Learning how to talk,
Getting rules from Mummy,
Learning how to walk.

Smiling and then screaming,
Eating sand and stones,
Imagine what you're dreaming,
Hear the adults' moans.

Now you are slightly older,
You will go to school,
You are getting bolder,
Sitting on a stool.

Now you have a job,
Now you understand,
Not a lazy blob,
Instead you own some land.

Now you have an illness,
Chance of living naught,
So you will pass away,
*And life's too short!*

**Jack Brook (7)**
Oakfield Prep School


## Zebra - Haiku

The lovely zebra
Is eating my vegetables
On the light green grass.

**Maria Pittas (8)**
Oakfield Prep School

## Sunny Places

Boiling beaches that are very hot,
Delicious peaches there are a lot.
Lots of fish are in the sea,
Come and have a swim with me.
Angelfish and lots, lots more,
Down on that cold ocean floor.
I drink cool coconut milk,
My clothes are made of electric-blue silk.
But I miss my home and the milk is very rich.
I don't like the silk it's too much of an itch.
So I think I will stay at home.

**Henry Jiao (8)**
Oakfield Prep School


## I Wonder

As I sit amongst this ice
So cold, so bitter
I watch these penguins waddle along
I wonder, I wonder
Why do they shuffle by
Instead of walking like you or I?
I wonder, I wonder
I wonder if these penguins
Are as cold in the ice as me
Of if they're just waddling home
To have their penguin tea.

**Hannah Warren-Miell (8)**
Oakfield Prep School

## The Star

One cold, dark night
Something was shining bright
In this holy town
There wasn't a sound.
In Bethlehem
There was a star as bright as a gem.

This star guides; guides to
Someone very special.

Mary and the little lambs
The shepherds and the three wise mans,
And Joseph and the baby King.
Hark! Let us sing.

This stars guides; guides to
Someone very special.

**Sahara Patel (9)**
**Oakfield Prep School**


## The Roman Army

The Roman army
are quite barmy,
and when they're bored,
They chop people's heads off with a sword,
and so,
they have to go
to the Roman hospital ward.

When the others go to battle,
the rest go and feed the cattle!
And when they found Greenland,
they took over England,
. . . and made a rock band!

**Angus Simpson (8)**
**Oakfield Prep School**

## The Land Of Wonder

I trooped through the woods,
Through the woods I saw a glittery, shiny round shape.
I didn't know what it was.
It seemed transparent
Then *puff!* But this puff was strange.
It didn't have a speck of dust or smoke, just stars.
There was so much light!
I could not see
Then it vanished.
All in my vision was the
Shimmering lake.
*Boom!*
I heard a voice,
'Shaun,' for that was my name.
'I-I-I c-c-come f-from t-t-the l-l-land of W-wonder.'
'What is the land of Wonder?' I whispered.
I seemed to be fixed to it or him,
I seemed to know him.
Then I saw his eyes,
Deep green and hypnotizing, he replied,
'Beyond your imagination, boy!'
Then I walked up, up and up.
Clouds and gold everywhere! I saw the sun.
*At night,* I thought, *how strange.*
I seemed in a trance,
The sun got bigger and bigger.
I saw a floating door, I opened it.
I entered the land of Wonder.

**Talia Yilmaz (9)**
**Oakfield Prep School**

## Cats And Poachers

Cheetah, cheetah watch him run
He's the fastest cat I know
If he sees the poachers come
He can run and run and go.

Tiger, tiger watch him flow
He's the coolest cat I know
If he sees the poachers come
He will jump upon their gun.

Lion, lion watch him roar
He's the most royal cat I know
If he sees the poachers come
He will blend with jungle growth.

Poacher, poacher watch him fall
He's the meanest man of all
Cats should seek them for their prey
It would serve him right each day.

**Nathanial Campbell (9)**
Oakfield Prep School

## Brothers!

I hate my brothers!
I wish they would stop fighting!
I wish they would stop screaming!
Oh and should I mention the biting?
When I tell them to leave my room it isn't any good!
They have never understood!
They make so much trouble!

Just let me say one more thing!
When will they ever learn?

**Amira Hasan (10)**
Oakfield Prep School

## Skin Deep

I always wear black mascara,
it's funky and cool to use,
it goes well with everything,
black mascara has nothing to lose.

Eyeliner's great at parties,
it makes you look slick and right.
The boys will say, 'Oh Mama,
wear that stuff tonight!'

Eyeshadow's classy,
it glitters and sparkles.
It's snazzy and groovy,
it's dazzlingly great.

Rosy cheeks are perfect,
blusher's simple and easy to wear.
Some blusher'll get you going,
use strawberry if you dare.

The lips are the most important,
if you want your looks to kill.
Gloss goes with glitter, it's glorious, it's glam,
you'll look like an angel, you will.

**Ruth Eliot (10)**
**Oakfield Prep School**


## The Cheetah - Haiku

The cheetah is here;
Spots flashing by in a whirl,
People stare in awe.

**Doris Dow (9)**
**Oakfield Prep School**

## Homework O' Homework

Homework o' homework
It isn't much fun
You have to sit down and do it
until it's all done.

Homework o' homework
Mum bosses you around
And if you don't do it
A detention will be found.

Homework o' homework
It's fun in the end,
'Cause once you've finished
You can play with your friend.

**Gabriel Agranoff (8)**
Oakfield Prep School

## Cats Everywhere
*(Based on 'Cats Sleep Anywhere' by Eleanor Farjeon)*

Cats, cats everywhere,
one by the stair,
one on a chair,
one is black,
one is white,
one is cool,
one is funny,
one is cuddly
and the rest are scruffy.

**Victoria Ewen (9)**
Oakfield Prep School

## The Silly Blackbird

There was a blackbird who was very concerned
About the man on the moon.
So the very next day, very tall, very straight,
He started his take-off run.
Oh yes! It was far so he decided to take a car.
Oops! No petrol in the car so he decided to give it a rest.
The very next day, he was off to the moon,
He tried a rocket and looked in his pocket
For the big heavy key but it wasn't there.
So in despair he decided to drop it.
So that is the end, he now has money to spend
And he will be back at half-past one.

**Christina Dwebeng (9)**
Oakfield Prep School

## Worms - Haiku

I wriggle around
Keeping the soil nice and fresh
Just doing my job.

**Rhiana Brown (8)**
Oakfield Prep School

## Winter - Haiku

All the frosty snow
Sitting on the trees and grass
Like a white blanket.

**Peter Leigh (8)**
Oakfield Prep School

## The Dead

They are the dead,
They no longer roam these lands.
Daisies fall from mourners' cold hands.
Arched, grey stones in a pretty field,
The smell of roses, tries to lift,
The perpetual cloak of solemn darkness and musty, breezy feel.
In the silence the church bell's dark peal
Carries on its low and dark chiming with great unease.
Suddenly, a flutter of wonder, a streak of misty sunshine
Through the pink and white blossomy trees;
While black as blackbirds the dead trees creak in time.
And not to be missed below is the long-forgotten grey
Over the dewy, soft grass,
Being trodden on by the silent people who pray.
People in black suits and gowns, cascading towards their feet,
Look miserably at the shiny box, in the new manmade ditch,
Showing no signs of a welcoming greet . . .
A dark silhouette, a shadow lies,
Over a grave, his spirit dies.
Then it's empty, once again,
Like a night so dark,
But in a misty glen.
It is dead,
It no longer roams these lands.

**Koray Yilmaz (11)**
Oakfield Prep School

## That's Not Like Me

Today is a school day,
People hate school, but that's okay.
I like school but sometimes I get in trouble but not all the time.
I cheat in games, but you have to win some time.
When I borrow something I sometimes don't return it.
But if you look at those things and then you look at me,
You will see that's not like me.

**Simisola Odimayo (9)**
Oakfield Prep School

## Tramps

We feel sad, but yet we do nothing,
But are grateful we aren't them.

They feel sad and they do nothing,
Not even get a job.

The government feels sad, they do nothing,
Not even help them off the street.

Who are we to blame?
We know the ones to thank.

Charities feel sad, they do everything,
Even give them homes.

If we were all good to each other
There would be none of them.
       Tramps.

**Rachel Williams (9)**
**Oakfield Prep School**


## My Favourite Things

I like animals all cuddly and cute,
I like the trumpet, the violin and the flute,
I like holidays in the sunny south west,
Devon and Cornwall are really the best.
I like my teddy bear, all fluffy and warm,
to cuddle and hold in a thunderstorm.
I like to play with my sister all day
with paints, paper, pens and clay.
I like the cat that lives next door,
although I've heard she chases mice across the floor.

**Annabel Norris (9)**
**Oakfield Prep School**

## A Bee

A bee!
A bee!
Is after me!
And that is why
I flee!
I flee!
This bee
This bee
Appears to be
Very, very
*Angry!*

**Nagawa Kabanda (9)**
Oakfield Prep School

## Fire

Fire, fire, sizzle, crack, in a nice cosy home
All the colours, orange and blue,
The smoking chimneys in the cold night air.
I sit alone and stare, stare, stare.
Fire, fire, sizzle, crack.

**Joshua Martin (8)**
Oakfield Prep School

## Aliens - Haiku

Are there eyes staring
beyond our solar system
out there in deep space?

**Emma Janusz (8)**
Oakfield Prep School

## Seasons

The spring brings daffodils
Tulips too
The sun starts shining
And the sky is blue.

The summer brings green grass
And a happy yellow sun
Summer is a jolly time
For laughter and fun.

The autumn brings lots of leaves
Red, yellow and brown
The leaves start falling from the trees
Down, down, down.

The winter brings us lots of snow
Oh no, no, no,
It makes our cars go very slow,
And Santa says, 'Ho, ho, ho.'

**Rachel Rawlinson (9)**
Oakfield Prep School

## Special Seasons

Special seasons are great!
They bring joy to the whole wide world
When special seasons come, there are smiles on people's faces
Everybody cheers
Everybody shouts, 'Special seasons are here!'
When special seasons are over everybody goes home
But still they had a great time, and so did the special seasons.
Now it is over!

**Drewe Williams (8)**
Oakfield Prep School

## The Blizzard's Creature

The sun was up
And shining through the land.
Herds of sheep grazed on pleasant grasses
Though on the other side of the lands
Snow glided on the wind,
Rain turned to hail
And water froze in the midst.
Birds flew here thinking it was warm
But flew right back faster than a rocket.
Polar bears became lazy
Because all they had to do was
Cut open the frozen ice.
Seals roamed the parts that were not frozen.
Seals starved and seals died.

**Hamish Cooper (10)**
Oakfield Prep School

## A Nonsense Poem

Elizabeth never told lies
Although she sometimes ate flies
I never understood
Why she always wore a hood
But it was always a great surprise
She played funny games
And never called people names
Even when she was very
Upset
She was always happy
And never wore nappies
But she always wet the bed.

**Freya Cooper (8)**
Oakfield Prep School

## Mother

Mothers know when you are faking
Mothers are the only people who can send hugs through the post,
Can do running repairs on the run.
Mothers tell the truth even if it hurts,
Mothers know when you're down in the dumps
And have that magic remedy to perk you up.
Mothers will always have a kind and caring word
To encourage and motivate you.
Mothers are awesome, what would we do without them?
*I love my mum!*

**Lauren Wilmott (10)**
**Oakfield Prep School**


## Christmas

Christmas is the time to
Be with your family and
Loved ones and share all the wonderful food.

Christmas is also the time to
Think about other people
Who are not in very good health like yourself.

Christmas is also the time
When you have to be kind
And very loving towards everyone.

**Jade Hermann (9)**
**Oakfield Prep School**


## Snow

Snow is white and falls from the sky to the ground.
Snow is for children to play snowball fights and build snowmen.
It is for snowboarding and skiing.
Snow is special because without snow we will be bored.
So remember that snow is important for having snowball fights.

**Jamal Edwards (9)**
**Oakfield Prep School**

# Hallowe'en

Double, double, toil and trouble
Potions flow and cauldron bubble,
Top of the green and yellow cake
Into the cauldron, bubble and bake.
Eye of snake and toe of frog
Wing of bat and wooden log
Black bat's bite and pink worm's sting
Red snake's fang and the magic ping
For a trick of powerful magic
Do some witches know some logic?
Double, double toil and trouble,
Fire burn and cauldron bubble,
Bang the witch's slimy wood
Then the potion's calm and good.
Witches' hats all grey and black,
Put their slime balls on a rack,
Cackle's date is Frankenstein tonight,
Vampire showed at the party with a fright.
The witches brew up sleeping potion,
While little soldiers spray magic lotion.
The witch's cat slides on a broom
Round and round the gloomy room.
The spider's web is very sticky,
The Devil's friend's name is Death from Ricky.
Frankenstein wakes up the dead
While shivering people go to bed.
Vampire sucks the dark, red blood
While witches add the ingredient, mud.
Frankenstein's skin is green.
Welcome to a creepy and gloomy Hallowe'en.

**Zein Harb (10)**
**Oakfield Prep School**

## The Storm

The storm is like a little devil,
As the rains are like little pieces of gravel.
When the time comes the Devil will strike
Like thunder with its trident,
While the gravel gives a strong scent.
The Devil will roar with ultimate fury
So if you anger the Devil you will be sorry.
The strong gales will blow your mails.
The gales will stop any sails.
Electricity will be delayed,
While the workers get paid.
In the garden children howl
To sleeping little baby owls.
Rain, rain, go away
Come again another day!
When parents are at work
The children will start to smirk.
Now the sunshine angel's here,
The Devil will be sure to be back.

**Samuel Kong (11)**
**Oakfield Prep School**

## Sea Horse

Sea horse, sea horse
Skin is quite coarse
Hides among the sea grass
Then crabs just pass
I saw it with my own eyes
It's as if it flies.

**Ayesha Ellis (8)**
**Oakfield Prep School**

## The Fall

Speeding like lightning,
You can't see me in a glimpse.
Rolling down ramps
With wheels glistening like diamonds beneath my feet -
Rising like a gliding Matisse.
I ollie in the air as high as can be
And kick-flip all day
Making vaerial flips over rainbows.
I grind till I drop
And then I come up with a plot -
To ride on the wall or scoot on the rocks . . .

I trip and I fall.
Was I butted by a bull?
180°d around to see what was there,
Not a bull or a cow or even a mouse,
But the wretched, hard-hearted enemy of the skater
That crack in the pavement, to me is a crater!
Cursed chip you're a skater hater.

I lie there wounded,
Upturned deck, wheels all buckled and bruised,
Axles glinting in the moonlight.
But
A skateboard I am,
So got up and rolled away -
Ready to skate another day.

**Kiman Xavante Hammond Read (11)**
Oakfield Prep School

## Special Days

Some days are special,
Some days are not,
Some days you get little,
Some days you get a lot,
Some days are hot,
Some days are not,
Some days you walk,
Some days you talk,
Some days you eat with a fork!

**Tara Collier (9)**
Oakfield Prep School

## The Ocean

There's a glow in the early morning
When the breeze comes flowing at you
With the scent of a passer-by.
You can't wait to get dressed and run out through the door
To see the ocean there as it awaits you.
'Time for school,' your mum shouts out the window.
'Get out of those clothes,' she says, rushing around.
You walk back in disappointment, looking back on yourself.

**Shanice Saunders (9)**
Oakfield Prep School

## The River Medway

The River Medway . . .
My currents flow, deeply coiling and curling,
Trapped under the boats feeling suffocated,
While they chugged and rumbled on the surface of me,
I felt as calm and loose,
The boats bobbed over the waves,
Like wild horses jumping over show jumps,
Coming first place,
First place.
The River Medway is in a dull swaying mood today,
My boat's turned and twisted and shone as the sun gloomed
And smiled at the River Medway.
The River Medway returns and smoothly disappeared
Out of shore once again.
The boats reflected as they painted a picture
With the colours of the water.
The River Medway, how wonderful.

**Brooke Hall (11)**
Perrymount Primary School

## Writing As The Arrows

The arrows flying through the air *smash, thud, bang!* All hit.
Reload and try again, *smash, thud, bang!* All hit the golden eye.

All at once arrows going everywhere on the target
Flying through the air all different colours
Flashing until they hit, *smash, thud, bang!*
Some hit the sheet and crash to the ground,
Most flying like golden eagles and then hit the target.
Targets now full of holes and arrows are still shooting,
*Smash, thud, bang!*
Finished and it is now time to collect the arrows and reload.

**Nikki Thompson (10)**
Perrymount Primary School

## The River Medway

                The river Medway
          A never-ending piece of rope
        Swaying, coiling into the sea
     As boats ride on the smooth surface
  Waves are left, rippling in place
Changing colour under the sky
As if a remote control was held in a bird passing by.

The river Medway
   Going out shore, and back in again
      Every time leaving treasures on the beach
        As the river holds parked boats
          The weed and sand stick to the bottom of them
       Army boats speeding on HRM part of the river
   Waves from underneath the boats
Spring up, and topple them.

The river Medway
   Is a calm place to be
      Sit on the wall overlooking the river
        With the breeze in your face

           Yes, the river Medway is the place to be.

**Necla Diker (11)**
**Perrymount Primary School**


## The Top

Higher than a tree
and bigger than me
lower then the sun
and taller than my mum
the rope is steady
so I am really, really ready.
Most people made it
to the top
others didn't
and had to stop.

**Jordan Stephenson (10)**
**Perrymount Primary School**

## The Climbing Wall

The wall, the wall,
Rough and high,
Climbing to the top,
Scary and tall.

The wall, the wall,
I'm terrified, shaking,
As I think I'm going to fall,
But I climb on,
When I hear my mates call.

Climbing like a monkey,
I'm feeling really proud,
As I climb the coloured rocks,
I reach the top,
I feel as high as a cloud.

**Poppy Franklin (10)**
**Perrymount Primary School**


## The High Ropes

A never-ending pole
A tight silvery wire
Keep on climbing
Don't stop
Don't give up
Scary
Frightening
Anxious
Worried
Past the rough rope
Onto the tight, hard bars
Stinging the palm of my hand.

**Joe Sutherland (11)**
**Perrymount Primary School**

# A Poem About A Mocktail

My drink is like a deep silvery mirror,
Looking straight at me,
As though I'm in it already.

> Looking at me face to face,
> As though it's actually alive,
> I see it bobbing out at me,
> Like a bouncy ball on my side.

My drink's going up and down like a yo-yo
I see it flying through the air
Although I just want to slurp it all up
I just don't care.

> As shallow as a swimming pool
> As lovely as a bear
> As red as lipstick
> On somebody's bright white hair.

Colours like rainbows
Red, orange, green and blue
It's all so sticky
Like a pot of glue.

> As I drink it down
> I have a funny feeling in my throat
> I see a reflection of me again
> Like I am inside a boat.

**Mergime Shala (11)**
**Perrymount Primary School**

## Bow And Arrow

First try, miss
Second try, hit
Third try, bullseye

A golden eagle soaring
Through the air,
Flying quicker and quicker
Every second.

First try, miss
Second try, hit
Third try, bullseye

The arrow plunges forward,
The elastic twanging,
Thud, outer ring
Thud, inner ring
Thud, got it!

First try, miss
Second try, hit
Third try, bullseye

Bullseye,
Bullseye,
Miss,
Hit,
*Bullseye!*

**Monique Francis (10)**
**Perrymount Primary School**

## The Target

The target
White, black and blue
Red and then gold
An arrow on the floor
Disappointment

The target
White, black
And an arrow on blue
Red and then gold
I try again

The target
White, black and blue
An arrow on red
And then gold
I try again

The target
White, black and blue
Red and . . .
*Bullseye* on the gold
Excitement.

**Fay Simpkiss (11)**
Perrymount Primary School

## Archery

Pointing by the target
Speeding through the sky
Pull the bow back
Using tight grip
Twack! Bullseye
Target reached.

**Max Gallant (10)**
Perrymount Primary School

# On The High Ropes

On the high ropes,
Staring down,
Minute figures,
Looking at me,
As the wind brushes against my face.

On the high ropes,
Trying not to look down,
As my legs tremble,
Walking along the smooth wooden platform.

On the high ropes,
Staring down,
Minute figures,
Looking at me,
As the wind brushes against my face.

On the high ropes,
My adrenaline running through my body,
Crawling up the metal staples,
Hoping not to drop.

On the high ropes,
Staring down,
Minute figures,
Looking at me,
As the wind brushes against my face.

**Shaun Johnson (11)**
**Perrymount Primary School**

## My Magic Box
*(Based on 'Magic Box' by Kit Wright)*

I will put in my magic box . . .

A river flowing backwards into the unknown,
The Milky Way,
A super car about to have turbo boost,
A waterfall filled with golden fish
Dancing the night away.

I will put in my magic box . . .

Another planet no one else knows about,
A star so bright it will glitter during the day,
A paradise just for me.

**Scott Kirby (9)**
St Mary Magdalen's Catholic School

## My Mum Katherine

You're like a flower in the garden,
You're like honey, sweet in my mouth,
You're like a teddy, always there for me to cuddle,
You're like a medicine that makes me well.

You're like a jacket keeping me warm and cosy,
You're like a golden sun shining upon me,
You're like an angel protecting me at night
And like a star looking at me from the sky.

**Margaret Obolo (9)**
St Mary Magdalen's Catholic School

# My Magic Box
*(Based on 'Magic Box' by Kit Wright)*

I will put in my box . . .

The wonders of the world.
A massive roaring cat.
A special flowing lake.
A working classroom.

I will put in my box . . .

A mansion for my family and I.
A busy school.
A large limo.
A marketplace filled with fruit.

I will put in my box . . .

The whole of New York.
A grassland filled with mud.
One hundred boiling deserts.
Five million pounds.

I will put in my box . . .

A beautiful ballet dancer.
A dangerous diving whale.
A golden coin glittering in the lake
And a hidden temple.

**Abigael Olorode (8)**
St Mary Magdalen's Catholic School


# Anger

I'm full of rage
I shouldn't have, couldn't have
My face is red and puffy
Why should I say sorry?

**Nakeitha Monguasa (9)**
St Mary Magdalen's Catholic School

## The Magic Box
*(Based on 'Magic Box' by Kit Wright)*

I will put in the box . . .
A hamster dancing in the night,
A genie painting itself green,
A secret diary opening and closing,
A magical coin glowing brightly,
A river slowly going backwards,
A flying carpet rocking backwards and forwards,
A pot of shapes jumbling themselves up,
A seashell making sounds of the sea,
Multicoloured pencils making a rainbow
And my family having a great time!

**Ashlé Suckoo (9)**
St Mary Magdalen's Catholic School


## Nan

You're the baby-blue drift of the sky
With clouds whirling around.
You're the sad song of Titanic -
But your soft tears comfort me.

You're the trees swaying this way and that
You're the Caribbean, full of heat
You're fried plantain -
Sizzling in a pan.

**Laurinda De Sousa (9)**
St Mary Magdalen's Catholic School

## When I Grow Up Will There Be?

When I grow up will there be . . .
Cherry blossoms on the tree,
Will they be waiting just for me?

When I grow up will there be . . .
Rosy red apples on the tree,
Will they still be waiting just for me?

When I grow up will there be . . .
Juicy yellow pears on the tree,
Will they also be waiting just for me?

When I grow up will there be . . .
Nice green London,
Will it be waiting just for me?

**Kate Lodge (9)**
St Mary Magdalen's Catholic School

## Dad

You're a fresh red Arsenal kit
Waiting for me to put it on.
You're a cold Fanta
Cooling me down after a kebab.
You're the new pair of trainers
I got for Christmas.
You're a pizza for supper.
You're Dad.

**Christopher Douglas (9)**
St Mary Magdalen's Catholic School

# The Magic Box
*(Based on 'Magic Box' by Kit Wright)*

I will put in the box . . .

Three golden sparkles of three golden stars,
the earth patterned with the sun and moon,
white light dazzling the clouds,
flowers dancing and singing in a chorus.

I will put in the box . . .

Glistening snow not melting in the vibrant sun,
shining wishes coming from little children,
fresh, green grass on purple flame - but not burning,
strong tastes and wonderful smells.

I will put in the box . . .

The silvery wind scattering pollen,
chirping birds with multicoloured songs,
trees bearing golden and silver fruits,
rain pouring down from the white, woolly clouds.

**Andrea Grillo (9)**
St Mary Magdalen's Catholic School

# My Uncle John

My uncle John, you are like a drink frozen in the fridge,
You are like my dad, taking care of me,
You are my bath, warming me,
You are my teacher, teaching me,
You are my friend, playing around with me,
You are the sunshine, shining on me.

**Denzel Uba (8)**
St Mary Magdalen's Catholic School

# My Magic Box
*(Based on 'Magic Box' by Kit Wright)*
I will put in the box . . .

A gleaming paradise just for me,
A streak of lightning and loud thunder,
The sweet smell of roses filling the air.

I will dance in my box
With the musical notes flying around me,
I will put in Mount Everest
So that I can climb it any time I want.
I will put in my box the Great Wall of China,
With you the reader walking along it.

In my box there will be . . .
The waves of the sea roaring ragingly,
Sausages in a pan bubbling and spitting,
The first word of a wonderful baby.

Somewhere in my box there's a carpet
Floating with Aladdin on it.
All my favourite stories are in my box
And most of my favourite feelings too.

**Sharma Beaton (8)**
St Mary Magdalen's Catholic School

# Grandma
You're the star that shone brightly at me.
You're the angel who sang to me.
You're spaghetti in my bowl.
You're there when I need you the most.
You're a tropical drink.
You're my woolly blanket; soft and warm.

**Joanna Hernandez (9)**
St Mary Magdalen's Catholic School

## Magic Box
*(Based on 'Magic Box' by Kit Wright)*

I will put in the box . . .
A dancing dinosaur on a mountain top on a summer's night.
I will put the sun and moon in my box.
The whole world will go in my box.
I will put my favourite dreams in my box,
Every season will go in there.
I will put the choir in my box
And a smile of a newborn baby.
I will put a cowboy on a broomstick
And a witch on a black horse.
All the beaches and oceans will go into the box.
The highest mountain will go in my box
And the seven seas.
The winner of all races will go in my box.
All the authors and illustrators will go in there
And finally I will put myself in the box.

**Chloe McGivan (8)**
**St Mary Magdalen's Catholic School**


## Mum

You are the soft lilac rushes swirling around me.
You are the cool, refreshing Fanta,
Just waiting for me on the table.
You are the smooth piece of silk ready for me to touch.
You're the sweet sauce combining the food.
You are the soft, smooth snow on the ground
And covering the trees.
You're music to my ears.
You're home with the roaring fire and hot chocolate.

**Holly Mason (10)**
**St Mary Magdalen's Catholic School**

# Magic Box
*(Based on 'Magic Box' by Kit Wright)*

I will put in the box . . .
A tornado with gold and silver fruits,
Fire breathing cats with golden fur.

I will put in the box . . .
A snowman standing in the desert
And a cactus in the snow.

I will put in the box . . .
A green sun
And a yellow moon,
Blue stars
And a white sky.

I will put in the box . . .
A green and blue world,
All the animals and people,
All the fireworks and sparks
And the wishes of a king.

I will put in the box . . .
One red star
And a white wand,
All the friends in the world
And a violin playing a soft lullaby.

**Sophie Runnicles (8)**
St Mary Magdalen's Catholic School

## My Uncle Rick

You're brown and white.
You're like a lion roaring at the birds flying in the sky.
You're like hot, boiling water in my bath.

You're like the sun shining in the sky.
You're like a mechanic; all dirty and greasy.
You're like a nightingale, singing at dawn.

You're like a cherry on top of my ice cream.
You're Coca-Cola fizzing on my tongue.
Life wouldn't be complete without you.

**Jordan Lohan (8)**
St Mary Magdalen's Catholic School


## In My Magic Box
*(Based on 'Magic Box' by Kit Wright)*

I will have Britney Spears playing 'Oops I Did It Again'.
A smell of donuts from the seaside
And a box of chocolates.
Blue dinosaurs dancing around with green grass.
The lake calming down.
A mouse running around trying to escape.
The bark of a cat and miaow of a dog.
A chirp of a bird
And the dip of a stone thrown into the sea.
All the birds flying to catch the slugs and snails.

**Lauren Barnden (9)**
St Mary Magdalen's Catholic School

## The Magic Box
*(Based on 'Magic Box' by Kit Wright)*

I will put in the box . . .
The hoot of an owl flying across from window to window,
The barking of arguing dogs,
The roaring of the sea.

I will put in the box . . .
A snake slithering,
A hamster, the Prime Minister of Hamsterdam,
The best rock band, Busted
And a mouse.

**Aaron McDonald (9)**
St Mary Magdalen's Catholic School

## My Dad Justin

You're like a purple reindeer,
You're music which wants to make me dance,
You're like rice and stew,
You're my special parent,
You're like lemonade in my cup,
You're like my furry jumper,
You're like home sweet home,
You're like my friend.

**Hazel Nezianya (9)**
St Mary Magdalen's Catholic School

## No, It's Not Always What You Want!

It was a Saturday morning,
I rushed downstairs,
I looked out the window,
It was raining again,
For me that meant
No football!

I then asked my mum,
'What are we doing today?
Can we go swimming?'
She said,
'No, it's not always what you want.'

That day we went shopping
Then I said,
'Can we watch a movie now?'
She said,
'No, it's not always what you want.'

She took me to the barbers
When we got home.
I said,
'Can I watch the Arsenal match?'
She said,
'No, it's not always what you want.'

We then watched
The Sound Of Music.
I was bored
Then I said,
'Can I go to bed now?'
She said,
'No, it's not always what you want.'
So I stayed up all night.

**James Naylor (10)**
**St Thomas More RC Primary School**

# Because

I'm playing on the wall
And teasing my brother.
My brother is off the wall
And he is teasing me.
Then my dad comes along,
'Stop that,' he says.
'Why?' I say.
'Because,' he tells me.

I'm playing PS2
And arguing with my brother.
My brother is playing PS2
And he is arguing with me.
Then my dad comes along,
'Stop that,' he says.
'Why?' I say.
'Because,' he tells me.

I'm watching TV
And arguing over the channels with my brother.
My brother is watching TV
And he's arguing over the channels with me.
Then my dad comes along,
'Stop that,' he says.
'Why?' I say.
'Because,' he tells me.

I'm playing football in the garden,
Not arguing with my brother.
My brother is watching TV,
Not arguing with me.
Then my dad comes along,
'Stop that,' he says.
'Yes, I can argue with my brother,' I say.
'Why didn't you say 'why' like you usually do,' he says.
'Because,' I tell him.

**Daniel Hickey (9)**
**St Thomas More RC Primary School**

# Time To Do Your Homework

I'm sneaking to the TV remote,
When Mum comes round the corner and
Mum says to me,
'Time to do your homework.'
I knew she would say it,
And there's no butting Mum.
I sneak round the corner
To put my skates on,
And there's Mum waiting,
And she says to me,
'Time to do your homework.'
And I am too scared to say a word.
I press the button,
The PlayStation button,
And there's Mum standing behind me,
And she says to me,
'Time to do your homework.'
I sneak into the cupboard
And I get a chocolate,
I nibble into it,
And I think, *where's Mum?*
I finish the chocolate,
I do my homework, satisfied with my chocolate,
And there's Mum and she says, 'Well done!'

**Oliver White (10)**
St Thomas More RC Primary School

## Dad! Dad!

I enter the house
My brother runs up to me and takes my glasses,
'Dad! Dad!
Sam's taken my glasses.'
I run to the bathroom, lock the door,
'Dad! Dad!
Sam's kicking the door.'
I open the door, where's Sam?
'Dad! Dad!
I can't find Sam.'
I run to the garden,
There's Sam popping the swimming pool.
'You two behave or I will ground you for a month.'
'Dad! Dad!'
'What now?'
'Nothing.'

**Shona Healy (10)**
St Thomas More RC Primary School


## I'm Warning You

It's a Saturday afternoon,
And I'm getting a bit bored.
So I go into the living room.
There's a big glass vase on the coffee table.
I go to pick it up, when I hear a voice saying,
'Don't even think of picking that up!'
But I don't listen!
And I go to pick it up.
Mum yells at me and . . .
*Smash!*
The vase has smashed into pieces!
My mum says, ' *I warned you!*
*Now you're in big trouble.*
*Just wait till Dad gets home!'*

**Millie Comis (9)**
St Thomas More RC Primary School

## Me And My Brother

Me and my brother
We rush home from school,
I turn on the TV
And my brother pinches me,
So I pinch him back.
'Mum, she pinched me!'
'But he pinched me first.'
'Amy, you're just as bad as he is!'

It's dinner time and my mum is calling,
So we rush to the table.
He flicks a carrot at me,
So I flick a carrot back at him.
'Mum she flicked a carrot at me!'
'But he flicked a carrot at me first.'
'Amy, you're just as bad as he is!'

I'm getting ready for bed
When my brother turns the light out,
So I pull his hair.
'Mum, Amy's pulling my hair!'
'But he turned the light off first,'
'Amy you're just as bad as he is!'

**Amy O'Connor (10)**
St Thomas More RC Primary School


## Hallowe'en

Hallowe'en is a scary night,
I lock then bolt the shutters,
I go downstairs, turn out the lights,
And start to hear strange mutters.

I go to bed, I'm not alone,
I feel a presence near,
I hear a voice begin to groan,
I start to shake with fear.

**Matias Grez (11)**
St Thomas More RC Primary School

## The Magic Box
*(Based on 'Magic Box' by Kit Wright)*

I will put in the box . . .
A big, bright blue sky for the day,
A round cracker for the moon at night,
A street light as a lamp.

I will put in the box . . .
A snowman with a hat,
A dog with a coat,
A Barbie in a Christmas dress.

I will put in the box . . .
A lily looking at the sun,
A rose the colour of blood,
A daisy floating in the water.

**Yasmin Borg Ryan (11)**
St Thomas More RC Primary School


## Famous

Oh how I wish to be famous,
I'd meet celebrities from the top,
But I'm still a lonely janitor,
Dreaming and talking to my mop.

Oh how I wish to be a star,
Oh help me, Lord, to be famous,
But I'm sitting like the lamest
And I'm not gonna get very far.

**Alex Ahern (11)**
St Thomas More RC Primary School

## The Magic Box
*(Based on 'Magic Box' by Kit Wright)*

I will put in the box . . .

A shimmering sun shining on a summer's day.
A Chinese child chuckling in a chair.
A swim and surf in the sea.

I will put in the box . . .

A giggle from my grandad,
A nod from nutty Nan,
A cry from my baby cousin.

I will put in my box . . .

A mysterious memory.
An eggciting egg at Easter,
A first present from Father Christmas.

My box is night and day,
My box is fun and boring,
My box is full of friends and enemies.

**Danielle Gough (10)**
St Thomas More RC Primary School

## Oh! Ruler

Oh lovely ruler, you gleam in the middle of the night,
You bend and curl in the most flexible way,
You intrigue me in the most amazing way,
Your luscious lines are grand, cheap plastic
Tickles the fairest of skin.
Your long, white angles, sharp to the point,
Your plastic detail blows the smartest of minds,
You draw me straight lines,
I couldn't survive without your expert touch.

**William Purbrick (10)**
St Thomas More RC Primary School

## The Magic Box
*(Based on 'Magic Box' by Kit Wright)*

I will put in the box . . .

The warmth of a fire,
The snow of a cold day,
The flower of joy.

I will put in my box . . .

My happy holidays I shared with my family,
The sandcastles I made on the beach,
And the swim I had in the sea.

I will put in my box . . .

The aunties who died,
The laughter of a baby,
And a friend in a friendship.

**Emily Merrell (10)**
St Thomas More RC Primary School


## Autumn Time

Swirling, twirling, round we go,
Blowing, whirling high and low,
Crunchy, crispy, hard and soft,
Rattling, rustling, breaking fast,
Brown, yellow, green and red,
Beige, purple, orange and lime,
Cracking, pattering, small and big,
Breaking, smashing, fast and slow.

**Percie Edgeler (10)**
St Thomas More RC Primary School

## Autumn Leaves

I
love the autumn
leaves as they
swirl peacefully
down from the branches, I am there
watching. Time passes and more
leaves fall all day long, as
the people walk by the
leaves make a crispy cry and
lie flat, squashed into the
ground. They come in all sorts of
colours, browns, reds, greens and
yellows. They come in lots of
different types, some can be
large, some can be tiny, some can
be not too big or not too
small, too many to
name because they
are just so beautiful.

**Isabella Fayers (10)**
St Thomas More RC Primary School

## Love

You are my vision, you are my love,
You are my angel sent down from above.
You are my precious, you are my life,
I want us to be husband and wife.
Every morning I wake up, I think about you.
Wondering if you think about me too.
When I saw you it was love at first sight,
That's when I knew I found Mr Right.

**Catherine Diales (11)**
St Thomas More RC Primary School

## The Magic Box
*(Based on 'Magic Box' by Kit Wright)*

I will put in my box . . .
A heart full of love,
a lovely white dove,
and a sign from above.

I will put in my box . . .
The man on the moon,
Santa who will come soon
and a royal gold spoon.

I will put in my box . . .
The shine of a wave,
the monster in the cave
the smile you gave.

I will put in my box . . .
The toy that I had lost,
the crystal-clear frost
and what love can cost.

My box is white with a ribbon so tight,
and a spider that can bite.

**Frances Fitzgerald (10)**
St Thomas More RC Primary School

## Whose Hands?

Glove-wearer
Molar-taker
Pliers-holder
Hole-dagger
Teeth-cleaner
Chair-lifter.

**Callee Hart (9)**
Sandhurst Junior School

## My Mum

Daughter-cuddler
Coffee-pourer
Flower-planter
Dinner-maker
Bed-tucker
Clothes-hanger
Baby-cuddler
Phone-user
Make-up-applier.

Whose hands am I?

**Katie Weller (9)**
Sandhurst Junior School

## Handy Andy

Hammer-holder
Nail-banger
Noisy-driller
Wood-carrier
Steady-painter
Accurate-measurer.

Whose hands am I?

**Caitlin Lawford (10)**
Sandhurst Junior School

# My Dad

Wardrobe-maker
Drill-pointer
Hammer-smacker
Loft-builder
Wall-creator
Bedroom-maker
Wall-destroyer
Lock-fixer
Shoulder-patter.

Whose hands are these?

**Mark Muzzlewhite (10)**
Sandhurst Junior School

# My Mum

Food-cooker
Money-handler
Nappy-changer
House-cleaner
Child-smacker
Car-driver.

Whose hands are these?

**Balwinder Nazran (9)**
Sandhurst Junior School

## Kennings

Computer-typer,
Document-writer,
Food-maker,
Clothes-washer,
Bed-tucker,
Phone-picker,
Phone bill-payer,
Food-carrier,
Prayer-warrior,
Church-worker,
Room-cleaner.

*Answer: My mum.*

**Shebah Mimano (9)**
Sandhurst Junior School

## Kennings

Colour-chooser,
French hat-wearer,
Paintbrush-holder,
Picture-maker,
Museum-shower,
Portrait-painter,
Picture-seller,
Frame-giver.

*Answer: An artist.*

**Nicole Hemmings (9)**
Sandhurst Junior School

## Kennings

Picture-drawer,
Book-illustrator,
Magazine-maker,
Pencil-holder,
Idea-haver,
Fight-drawer,
Detail-giver,
Pencil case-carrier,
Monster-maker.

*Answer: A cartoonist.*

**Sean Thurkle (9)**
Sandhurst Junior School

## Kennings

Note-writer
Pencil-holder
Tick-marker
Finger-pointer
Book-giver
Ring-wearer.

*Answer: My teacher.*

**Jiselle-Loren Campbell (9)**
Sandhurst Junior School

## Kennings

Homework-maker
Board-writer
Finger-pointer
Work-marker.

*Answer: My teacher.*

**Tegan Scott-Dobbs (9)**
Sandhurst Junior School

## Kennings

Rope-glider
Wall-climber
Object-returner
Person-pusher
Bomb-thrower
Camera-holder
Password-decoder.

*Answer: A spy.*

**Christine Lyston (10)**
Sandhurst Junior School

## Kennings

Dough-kneader
Cake-maker
Bowl-mixer
Dinner-server
Flour-sprinkler.

*Answer: A baker.*

**Felicia Ayeni (9)**
Sandhurst Junior School

## Kennings

Neck-strangler
Death-bringer
Gun-holder
Club-beater
Costume-changer.

*Answer: An assassin.*

**Brian Corfield (10)**
Sandhurst Junior School

## Whose Hands Are These?

Warm-hugger,
Finger-shaker,
Child-beckoner,
Computer-typer,
Bat-player,
Cooker-user,
Oven-opener,
Light-out-switcher,
Make-up-putter,
Gift-giver.

*Answer: My mum.*

**Josephine Bourne (9)**
Sandhurst Junior School

## Kennings

Fist-fighter,
Brick--breaker,
Sword-wielder,
Preying mantis-user,
Dagger-thrower,
Numchuk-swinger.

*Answer: Ninja.*

**Jordan Sewell (9)**
Sandhurst Junior School

## Who Am I?

Secret-keeper
Co-operative-worker
Good-listener
Fun-maker
Who am I?

*Answer: My best friend.*

**Alana Watson (9)**
Sandhurst Junior School

## Who Is This?

Joke-cracker
Laughing-master
TV-appearer
Film-maker
Crowd-pleaser.

*Answer: Lee Evans.*

Face-pounder
Body-blaster
Big-decker
Powerful-puncher
Undefeated-boxer.

*Answer: Ricky Hatton.*

**Alexander Whipham (10)**
**Sandhurst Junior School**

## Whose Hands Are These?

Pencil-holder
Paint-smoother
Line-drawer
Sketch-maker
Picture-capturer.

*Answer: An artist.*

**Atalia Johnson (9)**
**Sandhurst Junior School**

## Kennings

Dancing-wiggler
Laughing-giggler
Little-jiggler
Fish-catcher
Back-scratcher
Honey-eater
World-beater
Who am I?

*Answer: Brother bear.*

**Giovanni Ogboru (9)**
Sandhurst Junior School

## A Doctor

Injection-giver
Temperature-taker
Brow-mopper
Chest-tapper
Stethoscope-carrier
Scalpel-wielder
Prescription-writer
Whose hands am I?

**Shanequa Hutchinson (9)**
Sandhurst Junior School

## Kennings

Wheel turner
Trophy holder
Air puncher
Ferrari driver
Whose hands are these?

*Answer: Michael Schumacher.*

**Lemar Whyte (10)**
Sandhurst Junior School

## Whose Hands Are These?

List-checker
Present-giver
Sleigh-rider
Gift-wrapper
Toy-maker
Who am I?

*Answer: Father Christmas.*

Switch-toucher
Wheel-steerer
Fast-flyer
Button-pusher

*Answer: A pilot.*

**Paul Mitchell (9)**
Sandhurst Junior School


## Whose Hands Am I?

Law-maker
Make-up-applier
Crown-wearer
Oil-user
Jewellery-employer
Order-giver
Wine-drinker
Goose-eater.
Whose hands are these?

*Answer: Ancient Egyptian pharaoh.*

**Kajol Nandhra (9)**
Sandhurst Junior School

# Kennings

Child-smacker
House-cleaner
Care-taker
Nappy-changer
Who am I?

*Answer: Mum.*

Switch-toucher
Wheel-steerer
Fast-flyer
Button-pusher
Whose hands are these?

*Answer: A pilot.*

**Martin Ereck (9)**
Sandhurst Junior School

# Kennings

TV-watcher
Work-doer
Car-driver
School-taker.

*Answer: Dad.*

**Zeynab Mohammed (9)**
Sandhurst Junior School

## Whose Hands Are These?

Law-maker
Make-up-applier
Crown-wearer
Oil-user
Jewellery-employer
Order-giver
Wine-drinker
Goose-eater
Good-ruler
Whose hands are these?

*Answer: Ancient Egyptian pharaoh.*

**Aliye Giritli (10)**
Sandhurst Junior School


## Who Is This?

Car-driver
Gun-shooter
Secret-keeper
Lady-chaser
Plane-flyer
Bomb-exploder.

*Answer: James Bond.*

**Romario Williams (9)**
Sandhurst Junior School

## Kennings

Mummy-hugger
Bottle-sucker
Toy-stealer
Bed-sleeper
Bubble-blower
Brother-lover
Noise-maker
Lovely-cuddler
Who am I?

*Answer: A baby.*

**Helen McGhie (9)**
Sandhurst Junior School

## Who Am I?

Kind-lover
Sin-saver
World-keeper
Son-giver
Message-sender
Die-blesser.

*Answer: God.*

**Stephanie Quirk (10)**
Sandhurst Junior School

## Guess Whose Hands These Are

Wand-holder
String-knotter
Rabbit-stroker
Silk-puller
Spell-spinner
Finger-pointer.

*Answer: A magician.*

**Lucy Ives (10)**
Sandhurst Junior School

# Who Am I?

Sin-saver
Kind-lover
Heaven-keeper
Bread-giver
Father-prayer
World-creator
Die-blesser
Who am I?

*Answer: Jesus.*

**Jade Johnson (9)**
Sandhurst Junior School

# Kennings

Rope-puller
Parrot-handler
Sword-wielder
Treasure-taker
Gun-shooter
Tattoo-wearer
Whose hands are these?

*Answer: A pirate.*

**Efa Gough (9)**
Sandhurst Junior School

# Kennings

Gadget-handler
Fast-driver
Smart-dresser
High-flyer
Who am I?

*Answer: James Bond.*

**Zephaniah Steadman (10)**
Sandhurst Junior School

# Mermaid

She was . . .

As generous as a rose
Tall as a shed
Her teeth are the crystals
The rocks are her bed.

Each swim brought a cheer
Each breath blew a breeze
Her laugh moved an ocean
Each tear made waves freeze.

Her hair was the sky
Her tail was smooth
Her skin was the moon
Her voice gave a groove.

**Ryan Thornburrow (9)**
Sherington Primary School


# Mermaid

She was . . .

As beautiful as a white swan
Tall as a shed
Her eyes were the sparkling moon
The weeds her bed.

Each song brought joy
Each breath blew a lullaby
Her laugh livened the ocean
Each tear made the fishes cry.

Her hair was swaying in the breeze
Her tail as lovely as seashells
Her skin as pale as clear paper
Her voice the whisper of a bell.

**Ozde Yarseven (10)**
Sherington Primary School

## Mermaid

She was . . .

As kind as a god,
As fast as a bolt,
Her eyes were the sun,
Her song brought seas to a halt.

Each splash brought a tidal wave,
Each breath blew a sigh,
Her laugh as soft as the ocean,
Each tear made the ocean cry.

Her hair was flowing like the sea,
Her tail as red as a butterfly,
Her skin was white as a blank book,
Her voice was a lullaby.

**Dean Terry (9)**
Sherington Primary School

## The Sea

The sea is a tumbling avalanche
That crashes against the rocks.

It moans and moans at night
By day it dives at passers-by.

The sea is like a devil
Who bears you a grudge.

**Gethin Edwards (10)**
Sherington Primary School

## The Door
*(Based on 'The Door' by Miroslav Holub)*

Go and open the door.
Maybe outside there's a robot,
Or an aircraft,
A different planet,
Or a magic spaceship.

Go and open the door.
Maybe a cat's driving a McLaren,
Maybe you'll see a Concorde flying,
Or a propeller,
Or a brother of a brother.

Go and open the door.
If there's a rainbow,
It will disappear.

Go and open the door.
Even if there's only flowers growing,
Even if there's the sun setting,
Even if nothing is there . . .
Go and open the door.

At least there'll be a pretty garden.

**Jack Beer (8)**
The Pointer School

## The Boy Who Hated Pork

There was a young boy from York,
Who hated pork.
His name was Billy,
He was quite silly,
He tried some pork
And lost his fork,
Poor old Billy he hated pork.

**Max Higgins (10)**
The Pointer School

## The Door
*(Based on 'The Door' by Miroslav Holub)*

Go and open the door.
Maybe outside there's
A magic forest,
Or a castle,
A planet
Or a magic sea.

Go and open the door.
Maybe you'll see a wizard,
Or an alien,
Or a ghost
Of a ghost.

Go and open the door.
If there's wind,
It will blow.

Go and open the door.
Even if there's only a pond drying,
Even if there's only the wind blowing,
Even if nothing is there,
Go and open the door.
At least there'll be some sun.

**Petter Austad (7)**
**The Pointer School**


## Mechanic

Car fixer
Spanner mad
Bike repairer
Screw driver
Wrench turner
MOT checker.

**Adam Grahame (10)**
**The Pointer School**

## The Door
*(Based on 'The Door' by Miroslav Holub)*

Go and open the door.
Maybe outside there's
A world of toys,
Or a wonderful flying carpet,
Or a glittering wishing well.

Go and open the door.
Maybe there's a cat purring,
Maybe you'll see a beautiful palace,
Or a queen
Of a queen.

Go and open the door.
If there's a sun
It will rise.

Go and open the door.
Even if there's only the raindrops falling,
Even if there's people tripping,
Even if nothing is there,
Go and open the door.
At least there'll be people talking.

**Ella Sofi (8)**
**The Pointer School**


## May Haiku

May is my birthday,
My birthday is wonderful,
I love my birthday.

**Rachel Chung (9)**
**The Pointer School**

## The Door
*(Based on 'The Door' by Miroslav Holub)*

Go and open the door.
Maybe outside there's a library,
Or a flying carpet,
A grumpy gnome,
A merry little robin.

Go and open the door.
Maybe a cute kitten is scuffing,
Maybe you'll see Cinderella with her prince,
Or a fairy,
Or a baby
Of a baby.

Go and open the door.
If there's a cloud
It will rain.

Go and open the door.
Even if there's only the cars going,
Even if nothing is there,
Go and open the door.
At least there'll be a burst of sun.

**Heleana Neil (7)**
**The Pointer School**


## When The World Was Saved

Back then when the world was fun,
Just now I wish for some sun.
Oh how I wish the world was a better place,
Couldn't a bowling ball hit me in the face?
Then one day a man came,
To get rid of all our troubles,
Took out his sword,
Sliced the dark lord
And lived in peace forever.

**Raphael Newland (10)**
**The Pointer School**

## The Door
*(Based on 'The Door' by Miroslav Holub)*

Go and open the door.
Maybe outside there's an elephant,
Or Father Christmas,
Or a scrumptious turkey.

Go and open the door.
Maybe cheetahs are chasing,
Maybe there's a jungle
Or a golden Labrador,
Or a dog
Of a dog.

Go and open the door.
If there's a storm
It will blow.

Go and open the door.
Even if there's only the paint drying,
Even if there's only the dead tree,
Even if nothing is there,
Go and open the door.
At least there'll be a noise.

**Nic Higgins (7)**
**The Pointer School**


## Billy

There was a chicken who lived in Philly,
He couldn't swim and was called Billy.
One day he went to a swimming pool,
He nearly tripped over like a fool,
He jumped in and landed on something that screamed –
'Ger off, Willy from Philly.'

**Anand Kukadia (11)**
**The Pointer School**

## The Door
*(Based on 'The Door' by Miroslav Holub)*

Go and open the door.
Maybe outside there's a beautiful butterfly,
Or a fairy,
A smelly rat,
Or a magic garden.

Go and open the door.
Maybe a cat is chasing a mouse,
Maybe you'll see a bathroom,
Or a robot,
Or a sister
Of a sister.

Go and open the door.
If there's a parrot
It will fly.

Go and open the door.
Even if there's only the sun shining,
Even if there's only the wind blowing,
Even if nothing is there,
Go and open the door.
At least there'll be some traffic.

**Lien Raets (7)**
**The Pointer School**


## Ratty The Cat

There was a cat called Ratty,
Who couldn't eat anything too fatty.
He used to feel sick,
After eating a stick,
Then ended up looking quite tatty.

**Danielle McErlean (10)**
**The Pointer School**

## Dolphins

There was a dolphin
His name was Phin
He liked eating fish
But not from a dish
Phin is grey and blue
His eyes are sparkly too
His skin is soft and shiny
His teeth are very tiny
He is a very fast swimmer
So some people call him Spinner
Phin jumps so very high
Then splashes into the shape of a tie
I love Phin so much
He makes me want to swim with him
Phin is always in my mind
He is ever so gentle and kind
Phin will always be in my heart
I hope we will never be apart.

**Banisha Patel (9)**
The Pointer School


## Your Life

Your life is based on everything,
Your luck, your passion and health,
So if you take in anything,
Then it'll harm your life and wealth.

So take a breath and don't sweat,
Take it easily in your stride,
Cos one day you will see
That life has its good side!

**Dionyves Martin (10)**
The Pointer School

# Life

Life is too short
To just stand,
You have to learn
What you have been taught,
To be the greatest of your land.

Your ambitions you must choose,
As your life grows shorter,
Or just stand and lose,
Your life will turn to water.

Nothing is the same,
Nothing will change,
When your life is full of shame,
You, yourself must rearrange.

Life is too short
To just stare,
You have to learn
What you have been taught,
Your next career might be near.

**Chloé Saleh (11)**
The Pointer School

# Haiku

Playing games is fun
PlayStation 2 and Gamecube
Lots of fun with friends.

**Richard Samuel (11)**
The Pointer School

# The Dragon Of Bat Palace

In the dark, sad tower
There lived a beast
Who longed for a flower
From a human feast.

Then one day a warrior came
With his sword and shield
Lance was his name
And he picked up a sword he could wield.

He rode to the beast's lair
His heart full of fear
He took out a sword ready to slay
Knowing this was his death day.

The beast said
'Bring me a flower
and I'll escape from this tower
and live in much more peace.'

Lance did as he was told
And was very bold
And the beast lived
In peace forever.

**Alexander Saleh (9)**
**The Pointer School**

232    *Young Writers - Once Upon A Rhyme South East London*

## The Garden Monster

He creeps around the garden shed
I'm scared that he might eat my head.
I peep around the window curtain
It's a monster I am certain.
I see a rustle in the trees
I hope it's just the buzzing bees.
Or is it the monster that I fear
Or maybe I've been drinking too much beer.
I see a shadow walking
I think I heard it talking.
I heard 'ooohh', I heard 'aaahh'
I hope it was the noise of a car.
I bravely went outside
And looked behind my slide
And there what did I see?
Tiddles the pussycat who belongs to me.
Oh Tiddles, you gave me such a scare
Why don't you come in and sit on your chair?

**Mikaela Bere (9)**
**The Pointer School**


## Captain Pizza Man

One day we went
To see the pizza man
But then we saw he was a fake
And was replaced by his uncle, Francis Drake.

He said, 'I'll fire a cannon at you'
So he got a match to fire a cannon
But he realized it had no gunpowder.

So he went to visit Guy Fawkes
'I want some gunpowder,' said Francis
'OK,' said Guy, 'that'll cost £100'
So he fired a cannon and he missed
Instead he hit an enemy's ship.

**Peter Currie (8)**
**The Pointer School**

# Fairies

The glitter fairy
Sparkling bright
Dancing her way
Into the night.
The dream fairy
Kissing goodnight
Giving you dreams
To your delight.
The joy fairy
Singing a song
Being happy
All day long.
The star fairy
Had a dance
She missed a fairy out
By chance.
The little fairy
Was invited
And guess what
She was delighted.
The kind fairy
Was there too
Everything she said
Was true.
The last fairy
Left at all
Was not invited
To the ball.

**Eva Conn (9)**
**The Pointer School**

## The Zoo

I went to the zoo
Guess what I saw?
A hippopotamus
And a dinosaur.

Next I saw a lion's den
They were feeding on a big fat hen.
A crocodile leapt up at me
He was smiling at his tea.
'A monkey, a monkey,' I said
With a big smile I led . . .

To the tiger
Its long tail
It looked like a slimy snail
It was time to go.

I said, 'Oh'
There was a sweet shop
I said, 'Can I have a sweet?'
Mum said, 'Those are not to eat.'

**Gabriela Saffer-Ford (8)**
**The Pointer School**


## With The Birds Haiku

Soaring to the clouds
Oh, flying high in the sky
Above all the birds.

**Matthew Dean (10)**
**The Pointer School**

## The Knitting Toad

One day
A frog was playing with some clay
Instead of sitting
He really should be knitting.

So he went knitting with his needle
Then did a little bit of tweedle
Oh please, not another load
Of knitting toads.

I've had enough of knitting toads
Just take some away, but don't leave loads
I'm leaving home
Oh no, not a gnome!

**Paola Delivre (8)**
The Pointer School


## Toad

Once upon a time a toad called Jim
Saw his friend trying to swim.
'Oh dear, I'm such a silly toad
I can't let my mate get crushed by a torpedo!'
So Jim suddenly jumped in
Then he realized he couldn't swim
'I can't let my Bill get crushed by this thingy
Still, lucky for me it's only . . . *croak*
But right now he is soaked!

**Huw Jones (9)**
The Pointer School

# Fairies

In the middle of the night
A little fairy flies up
With her sparkling dress shining bright
She soars up and up through twinkling stars
And strokes them with the tip of her wand.

The tooth fairy creeps around
Trying not to make a single sound
While you're snuggled up in bed
She pulls out a tooth
And knocks over your ted.

When it's raining at night
The rainbow fairy comes in sight
She makes a rainbow of seven colors
But oh no, she made a mistake
And flew away in horror.

When you're upset
The friendship fairy comes down
She gives you a hug
And sprinkles fairy dust
To make you feel better.

**Mandy Ma (8)**
**The Pointer School**

## The Longer Than Usual Nonsense Poem

There once was a man from Canada,
Who thought he was eating his bandana,
Awoken was he,
Was knee high in fleas,
But my poem is longer than that!

Then that itchy man from Canada,
Went to the local suntanner,
Though he got bored,
He glowed like a lord,
But my poem is longer than that!

Then that glowing man who was Canadian,
Was soon mistaken for an alien,
Then a spaceship shaped like a dove,
Beamed him above,
But my poem is a tiny bit longer than that!

Then that scared man from Canada,
Was caught when they saw his bandana,
The man was brave,
But soon after in his grave
And that is the end of my poem.

**Josiah Adojutelegan (9)**
**Thorntree Primary School**


## Colours Of The World

The sea is blue
Because it has the flu,
The grass is green
And this I've seen.

The robin's nest is brown,
It's in the tree that's in the town,
The bark is brown,
I can't hear a sound.

**Francesca Latamsing (9)**
**Thorntree Primary School**

## Tinker

My cat, Tinker,
Is a lovely cat,
A gentle cat,
A wild cat.

My cat, Tinker,
Is a good cat,
A home cat,
A sleepy cat.

My cat, Tinker,
Is a hungry cat,
Is a playful cat,
A funny cat.

I love my cat!

**Steven Walker (8)**
**Thorntree Primary School**

## Wish Dish

As big as a fish,
As small as a wish,
As funny as a clown,
As angry as a frown,
As crazy as a ball,
As mad as a fool,
As loud as a clap,
As quiet as a map.

**Louise Case (8)**
**Thorntree Primary School**

## My PS1

I have a PS1
It is loads of fun.

It's a game you can
Play on your own.

I play loads of games
And enjoy all the names.

I can even take it
Out in the sun.

I'm just like a dog with a bone
And don't mind playing alone
In fact, it's best if I am!

I can honestly say
That I am happy today
'Cause I've got my own PS1.

**Ross-Anthony Monteiro (9)**
**Thorntree Primary School**


## My Teacher's Pet

My teacher's pet is called Matt,
He always chews the chairs,
Tumbles down the tables,
Rules the rulers,
Punches the pencils,
Rubs the rubbers out
And dents the door!

**India Golding (9)**
**Thorntree Primary School**

## Nightmare

I had a nightmare in May,
But it was in the middle of the day.
I dreamt I went to the moon,
On a large teaspoon.
I saw a vamp
And he ran after me with a lamp.
I walked into a wall,
Then I fell in a pool.
I met a tiny cat
And then she turned into a mat.
Then I woke up in the middle of the day
And then . . .

**China Norris (9)**
Thorntree Primary School

## Life

Life - it's what we live,
And sometimes I like it,
Life is what we give,
All of us have one life,
To be happy with.

Life is a wonderful thing,
Life is a good gift from God,
We talk, shout and sing,
And sometimes life can be odd
And he gave a good life to the king.

**Hannah Newman (9)**
Thorntree Primary School

## Animals' Differences

Animals, animals everywhere,
Some that eat apples, some that eat pears,
It doesn't matter what they are,
As long as they don't drive cars!

Monkeys, tigers, African bears,
All these eat and breathe air,
Some cold-blooded, some warm blooded,
At least their homes haven't been flooded!

Toucans, birds, flying hawks,
Some fly and some walk,
Some short-sighted, some long-sighted,
Sometimes sad and sometimes delighted!

Lions, apes, swinging baboons,
All that eat breakfast but not with spoons,
Some meat-eaters, some not,
Some sleep in nests, some sleep in cots!

Penguins, polar bears, harp seals,
All that can move and feel,
Some that swim, some that walk,
Some that dig and some that talk!

**Ben Khoshnevisan (8)**
Thorntree Primary School


## September

Autumn is fun,
Conkers on the tree fall on the ground,
Play in the leaves,
All day long.

Acorns on the ground,
Squirrels run around and around,
Gathering them up for their winter feed.

**Melissa Laurence (8)**
Thorntree Primary School

## Going

Soon, *poof, kapow!* It'll all be lost.
All of it, like it never happened,
Cos I know how it all goes.
Goes being the operative word,
As that's what we're doing.
It's not as if it's being rushed.
We spent ages on it.
Still are.
It's our 'dream'.
But I suppose leaving London'll be
A 'new experience'.
It's leaving everything that'll be
The New Experience.
I don't want to.
But I do as well.
Wonder what it'll be like.
Better start packing.
Bye.

**Josie Rogers (9)**
**Thorntree Primary School**


## Animal Nonsense

Dogs bark,
Mice squeak,
Cats miaow
And I speak.

Lions roar,
But can't open a door,
Tigers can't roar,
But are faster than ever.

Fish can't speak,
But sometimes their tanks leak,
Tortoises are slow,
But sometimes they roll up like a bow.

**Nicholas Bulgen (8)**
**Thorntree Primary School**

## Words

I like words.
Do you like words?
Words aren't hard to find,
Words on walls and words in books,
Words deep in your mind.

Words in jokes,
That make you laugh,
Words that seem to smell,
Words that end up inside out,
Words you cannot spell.

Words that fly
And words that crawl,
Words that screech and bump and bawl,
Words that jump and words that slide,
They are the words that I like.

**Lucy Fair (8)**
**Thorntree Primary School**


## People

People with blonde hair,
People with brown,
People who are happy,
People who frown,
People with ginger hair,
People with black,
People who care,
People who share.

This world is full of different people,
Don't try and name them all.

**Holly Spencer (9)**
**Thorntree Primary School**

## Planets

Planets, planets, red, yellow and green,
Some hot, some cold and some the same.
Some gaseous and rock hard, with one thing the same,
They float in space.

Saturn, Uranus and Neptune,
Saturn big, Uranus medium and Neptune small.
All have rings, but Saturn lives with the most,
But Uranus and Neptune only have one.

Pluto, Earth and Venus,
Venus the hottest, Earth warm and Pluto cold,
All different temperatures, the Earth the best,
But Venus and Pluto are not alike.

Jupiter, Mars and Mercury,
Jupiter medium, Mars too, Mercury closest to the sun.
Jupiter with a red spot, Mars red all over,
But Mercury has no red at all.

**Trevor O'Connor (9)**
**Thorntree Primary School**


## The Sea

The sea is peaceful
The sea is quiet
The sea is moody
The sea is vintage
The sea is beautiful
The sea is overjoyed
The sea is colourful
The sea is clear
The sea is perfect
The sea is handy
The sea is suitable
The sea is special.

**Temidayo Olateju (9)**
**Thorntree Primary School**

# The Boiling Man

In the middle of the town
Where the ripe trees grow

Heating up leaves
And dying flowers

Children running
Getting thirsty

A blazing sun
Struck upon the town
A man running to work
On the burning floor

Burning heat
Burning heat

Here is a house of
Sunbathing chicks

Getting suntanned
Drinking iced tea

You understand
It's like a scared cat

Drinking, gulping
In every garden

When the boiling man comes to your door
Let him in for a drink

Let him in for a drink
Lemonade or iced tea.

**Damilola Nezianya**
**Thorntree Primary School**

## Can I Be?

Can I be, can I be
As tall as a tree
Or as small as a bee?

Can I be, can I be
As cute as a cat
Or as dirty as a rat?

Can I be, can I be
As clean as a mat
Or as scrufffy as a bat?

Can I be, can I be
As neat as Granny
Or as rough as Sammy?

Can I be, can I be
As smart as the sea
Or as dull as a flea?

Can I be, can I be
Just like me?
Oh, please let me be . . .

Me, me, me, me, me!

**Ndidi Aliago (10)**
Thorntree Primary School


## I Once Saw A Nerd

I once saw a nerd
Who turned into a bird.

I put him in a cage,
He began to turn beige.

I took him to the vet,
He said, 'What a strange pet!'

It must be a rare bird,
Then puff - it's a nerd.

**Elizabeth Hogg (9)**
Thorntree Primary School

# Questions

Do boys tire of football?
Do mums tire of phones?
Do girls tire of lipstick?
Do skeletons tire of bones?

Do dogs tire of balls?
Do cats tire of play?
Do mice tire of cheese?
Do horses tire of hay?

Do children tire of games?
Do people tire of walking?
Do brothers tire of girlfriends?
Do sister tire of talking?

Do cakes tire of icing?
Do fingers tire of picking?
Does hair tire of combs?
Do tongues tire of licking?

**Emily Grain (9)**
**Thorntree Primary School**


# Channels

On channel one it's dead boring,
On channel two it's snoring,
On channel three it's nothing but news,
On channel four it's nothing but a snooze,
On channel five it's golden rules,
On channel six it's nothing but jewels,
On channel seven it's nothing but clocks,
On channel eight it's a pair of old socks,
On channel nine it's all about me,
So I'd better flee.

**Jake Moore (9)**
**Thorntree Primary School**

## Questions

Are shoes tired of feet,
Are grannies tired of knitting,
Does fire tire of the heat,
Do clothes tire of fitting?

Do cats tire of purring,
Do birds tire of flying,
Do javelins tire of hurling,
Do eggs tire of frying?

Do Greeks tire of gods,
Do prisoners tire of cells,
Do people tire of dogs,
Do devils tire of the hells?

Do streets tire of cars,
I think everything gets tired!

**Callum Grant (10)**
Thorntree Primary School


## Peter Pan

There was a man called Peter Pan,
Who once returned to Never Land,
He had faith, trust
And pixie dust,
That made him go high,
So then he could fly.
Captain Hook came and took,
Poor young Wendy away.
He sailed the seas
And had Wendy tied up in a bag,
All she was dressed in was a little rag.
Peter Pan was the saviour,
Dressed in a pea-green suit,
He took Wendy home as he knew the route.

**Georgia Fair (10)**
Thorntree Primary School

## What I'm Good At

I like to play basketball,
I'm good at it, I don't lie,
I destroy the other side.

I like cricket,
Because I knock out batsmen
And hit the wicket.

I'm good at running,
I look stunning
Whenever I run around.

I like art,
I could draw Bart,
I'm good at art and I'm smart.

I like drawing,
It's not boring,
It's the thing I could do.

**Vishal Koria (9)**
Thorntree Primary School

## Snowflake

Snowflake, you gracefully fall to the ground
Snowflake, you twinkle in the moonlit sky
Snowflake, when you touch the ground you change
You change into a sparkling blanket
You're not a snowflake anymore
Children play with you now
You turn into ice, then into grey sludge
But you will come again next year, snowflake.

**Jessica McHugh (10)**
Thorntree Primary School

## The Mysterious, Black Creature

The mysterious, black creature
Roamed across the land,
Running away from its dark
And lonely shadow.

The mysterious, black creature
Was alone and in danger,
Yet it still decided to fend
For itself.

The mysterious, black creature
Felt so cold and strangely chilled,
That it finally knew what it felt like
To be an ice cube.

*Click*, the light switch whispered
To the air,
As the black creature rapidly leapt
Under a wooden, four-legged bridge.

As the light revealed itself
To the dark land,
The area slowly became
A modern kitchen.

The mysterious, black creature
Began to shrink in size,
And became a small
Grey-coloured kitten.

**Jane Adojutelegan (11)**
**Thorntree Primary School**


## Rabbit

Rabbit is an animal, a very jumpy animal.
Rabbit is a friend, who never gets out of bed.
Rabbits are fun, but are sometimes very dumb.
Rabbits have fur and are as soft as a chinchilla.

**Joseph Massey (11)**
**Thorntree Primary School**

## Roses Are Red, Violets Are Blue

Roses are red, violets are blue,
There's no one in the world
That matters as much as you.
You make me smile,
You make me sing,
You make me happy
With a ring-a-ding-ding.

You cheer me up on a rainy day,
You make me feel like a summer's day,
You fill me up with your love and joy,
You play with me like your favourite toy.

When I have a bad feeling inside,
You pass through and take it outside.
Most of all you're really nice,
You put a smile on my face.

**Hayley Carey (10)**
**Thorntree Primary School**


## I Know A Fly

*(Read quickly)*

I know a fly
I know a fly who wears a blue tie
I know a fly who wears a blue tie
His favourite food is a nice juicy pie
I know a fly who wears a blue tie
His favourite food is a nice juicy pie
That's the fly I know
I know a fly who wears a blue tie
His favourite food is a nice juicy pie
That's the fly I know
He has a big red bed
He has a bad enemy called Jed
That's the fly we know.

**Oscar Farmer (10)**
**Thorntree Primary School**

## My Sister, Grace

My sister, Grace, is a pain,
When she's bad,
I always get the blame.
She's very mad,
But I am glad,
Because she sometimes gives me the giggles.

She has got beautiful, golden curls,
And teeth like pearls.
Her favourite colours are blue and green,
Sometimes she can be really mean.

She's as strong as an elephant,
As small as a mole.
She's as brave as a lion,
But when it comes to a show,
She's as timid as a mouse.

Even when she gets on my nerves,
Deep down I know I still love her.

**Amy Bowden (10)**
**Thorntree Primary School**


## Teachers

Teachers, teachers,
Always moan,
Never happy,
But always groan,
They make you work,
As much as you can,
Teachers, teachers,
Sometimes happy,
Sometimes sad,
But whatever I do,
I'm always glad,
That Mrs Fayers is always around.

**Terri-Anne Morris (10)**
**Thorntree Primary School**

## My New Shoes

Well, my new shoes are shining and blue,
Made from cow's leather,
All the best cobblers gathered together.

My new shoes are long and pointy,
They're so sharp you could cut cheese,
Everyone wants to look like me!

So?
My new shoes were made in India!
They've got sequins, bindies and jewels,
When I first saw them I said, 'Mamma mia!'

Well, I've got boots,
Made of polar bear fur,
The only bad thing is,
I can only wear them in winter.

But I think my old ones are the best,
They may be tattered and bare,
But they get me everywhere!

**Yolanda Allen (10)**
**Thorntree Primary School**


## Dracula

In Transylvania where cruel things happen
Dracula awaits his prey
He's the face of doom
And has five hundred rooms
Dangerous and daring, evil and staring.

His teeth are like steel
He steps with no care
Even when the fire flames
Don't believe this creature
Hideous and ferocious, don't wake him!

**Lee Burton (10)**
**Thorntree Primary School**

## You Are The Sun

You are a yellow beach ball floating in the air.
You are a yellow ball that's always there.
You are a light shining that's very hot.
You never ever give up because you are so peaceful.
You're always there, especially here.
You look so bright, as the light.
You make me feel so good inside that I don't feel the need
to hide.
You are the sun.
You rise like a ball that's been thrown in the air.
You are so hot that I stay inside.
You are the sun.
You are so small that you look just like a beach ball.
You can never be cold but hot and bold.
You are the sun.

**Sonia Ahmed (10)**
**Thorntree Primary School**


## Snakes

Snakes are slimy, wet and cold
Lots are fearless, lots are bold
Their fangs are as sharp as a spear
Some snakes love eating deer
Some snakes are colourful
Don't believe it, even when you're gullible
Stay still
Don't be thrilled.

Snakes peel
Strong as steel
Some are harmless as daffodils
Snakes slither with their scales
And some are the size of whales
They also like to kill cows.

**Joe Perry (11)**
**Thorntree Primary School**

## Connor
*(In the style of Sonnet 18)*

Shall I compare you to a cheetah?
You are more speedy and more lively.
To me you're as clever as a genius.
In the County Championship
You are so agile you could dodge lightning
And swim with the dolphins.
Your eyes are ocean-blue.
Your hair is as brown as bark.
You can be so serious or very silly.
Your cheeks are as cheery as a crackling log fire.
You have more freckles than a giraffe.
You are as bold as the world's strongest man.
You are as cool as ice -
You are my friend.

**Tom Hopkins (11)**
**Thorntree Primary School**


## Red

Red is in your head
Red is with you when you're dead
Red is out when you're cut
Red is out when you're hurt
Red is everywhere
Red is inside you
Red is beside you
Red is inside you.

**Joel Moore (11)**
**Thorntree Primary School**

## Zoo Bars

I'm a crocodile
I've never walked a mile
Away from this zoo.
But there's nothing to do.
I want to run away
Because there isn't much pay,
Apart from some fish
Which aren't even on a dish!

I'm a lion,
I've only felt the iron
Of this old cage.
I've read every page
Of my books.
I'm better than those cooks,
Killing and eating,
Ripping and beating.

I'm a monkey,
I try to steal the key,
I want to get out.
I'd even pick a bout
With anyone in the way
Of me getting away.
I'd better get some food,
Before I really get in a mood!

**Simon Dodd Wild (11)**
**Thorntree Primary School**

# Witch

When my friend went green
And her ear began to itch,
Then she got a bit mean
And I knew she was a witch.

The witch went crazy
And soon went mad!
She was no lady,
And that was bad.

She went blue
And I went red,
This poem is true,
I was scared when I went to bed.

When she had black spots
I knew that was wrong,
Soon her spots began to pop
And I knew we would never get along.

I found a new friend
And he was my mate,
The chase had ended
And that was great.

**Jason Summerfield (11)**
**Thorntree Primary School**

## But You're Dangerous

You are like a blue beanbag
Floating in mid-air.
You are like my best friend
Because you are always there.
You are as cold as snow
You've got a good flow.
*But you're dangerous!*

You make a huge sound
I can hear you all around.
Your crash is so loud
You must be proud.
*But you're dangerous!*

Your touch is so nice
You are as cold as ice.
You can take lives
Without using knives
*And you are dangerous!*

**Ria Berry (10)**
**Thorntree Primary School**